IT CAME FROM THE KITCHEN

BY GEOFF ISAAC
&
GORDON REID

ARTWORK BY TERRY MARSH

Cover design and artwork Terry Marsh
©2006
www.methehead.com

Excerpts from *All I Need To Know About Filmmaking I Learned From The Toxic Avenger*
© 1998 Troma Entertainment, Inc.

A portion of the proceeds of the sale of this book will be donated to charities.

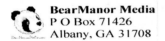
BearManor Media
P O Box 71426
Albany, GA 31708

TABLE OF CONTENTS

PASTA 85

POULTRY 107

FROM THE SEA 129

MEATS 149

DESSERTS 182

"LET THE FEAST BEGIN"
- ALBUS DUMBLEDORE (RICHARD HARRIS)
HARRY POTTER AND THE PHILOSOPHER'S STONE (2001)

FOREWORD

By Ingrid Pitt

It is often quoted that sex is the subject which most occupies the adult and post pubescent mind. Not so. Food is the number one theme that unites humanity. Even that sexed-up teenage boy lusting after the girls' netball captain gets his libido burnished with a nourishing hamburger while fantasizing their union. Different cultures — different partialities. France has long been voted the nation which does wonders in making unmentionable ingredients mentionable — and tasty. Italy goes for the sauce to make the pasta palatable. Germany does — er — well, sauerkraut while the Norwegians slaver over a colorful Smorgasbord. America has the image of a giant burger staked by a patriotic flag, Scotland goes for the messy business of a sporran full of porridge, while England's contribution to the hungry world is the fast-food industry. The Earl of Sandwich slapped a hunk of beef into a loaf of bread and there it was. The sandwich painted the atlas pink in the days of Empire. It still strides the film world in the shape of the Bacon Buttie. When the TV series *Sharpe* was being made in Russian regular lorry loads of bacon wended their way across Europe. By the time it reached its destination it was considerably lighter than when it started out and customs officials and freight handlers had developed a taste for Britain's gift to the world.

Entertainers have a great opportunity to sample the fare offered by national taste. As they move around from country to country, often visiting exotic and far-flung locations, they have a wonderful chance to indulge in the local specialities. Indian and Chinese food has spread throughout the world and is often what is most sought after by hungry crews. Except in Transylvania where slipping out for a Chinese, Indian or Big Mac has more sinister connotations.

Geoff Isaac and Gordon Reid have spent a lot of time rounding up the flavors which fuel the film industry. My personal choice leans towards the more esoteric although I have often found that a nice slab of cod and a heap of chips, deep fried in butter, wrapped in newspaper and eaten on Brighton Beach on a crisp Autumn night, hits the spot. One thing is for certain, if you try the recipes in *IT CAME FROM THE KITCHEN* you are sure of a satisfying gastronomic feast.

December 2006

PREFACE

This book is about passion for cooking and film-making; two disciplines requiring patience, skill, a collaboration of the right ingredients and the personal expression of their maker.

While there are films with food scenes that have left indelible memories, one would be hard pressed to find a movie where cooking plays a pivotal role in the plot. We would know as we spent nearly a year trying to find them all. Plots don't generally hang in the balance based on what a character chose to eat one day. This reality made the book you are holding somewhat harder to create.

As much as we love to write and cook, we are fans first and foremost. So we made lists of our favorite actors, writers, directors, make-up and effects technicians. Our requirement was that they made a contribution to the fantasy, science fiction or horror film and television genres in some respect. We didn't get too overly concerned about definitions. We focused on film and television since they have had the most profound influence on fans and popular culture.

We wrote letters, made phone calls and sometimes even visited— thanks to the marvel of conventions — our favorite actors, writers, artists and directors. We asked them if they had a recipe to send. In the event they did not have any, we asked them for their favorite foods or any food related stories. This lead to many surprising responses. Some, like Producer Herbert L. Strock and actor Doug Bradley gave us pages and pages of anecdotes. Others were less verbose. Martin Sheen sent us a signed photo and wrote "Cream of Wheat" below the signature.

It was important to us that as many creative capacities in film as possible were fully represented, and that all the genres be well represented in this book. If you find holes, or discover that your favorite star, writer or director is missing, know that we've probably made at least some attempt to include them. To those who opened their kitchen to us, we thank them.

It has been a long and laborious process, but a very rewarding one. When a contact did not have a recipe of their own, we asked our chefs to create a culinary masterpiece. We used the symbol "Our Pick" to denote these recipes. This book not only gave us the opportunity to connect with the people who have inspired us, but to make a difference by donating proceeds to some wonderful charities.

It was never our intent to simply create another addition to your cookbook shelf. Additionally, we hope this book will just as likely become an addition to your bedside table. At the very least, you'll have something to read while waiting for the water to boil.

Geoff Isaac
Gordon Reid

ACKNOWLEDGEMENTS

This book would simply not exist without the generous assistance of the following:

Lucy Chase Williams, Patricia Hitchcock, Ron Chaney, Bela G. Lugosi, Sara Karloff, Victoria Price, Arianna Ulmer Cipes, Donald Fearney, Sue Cowie, Colin Cowie, Ted A. Bohus, Norma Dolan, Greg Turnbull, Ron Adams, Dick Klemensen, Gary Dorst, Ron Borst, Mike Murphy of Dark Terrors, Joyce Broughton, Mike Searle, Bob Searle, Richard Zahn, Jamie Proctor, Scott Hughes, Ted Newsom, Steve Jones, Michael Anderson, Lloyd Kaufman and Troma Entertainment, Malia Howard, Bob King, Harry Knowles, Emily Duncan, Kevin Clement at Chiller Theatre, Pierce Jensen, Dave Brethour, Jon Heitland, Gary Svehla, Sue Svehla, Kasey Rogers, Dee Ankers Denning, Donna Neuman, Michael Lennick, Michael Levine, David Fortier, Mike Hodges, Terry Marsh and Ingrid Pitt.

Special thanks to Joseph Stefano and Irvin S. Yeaworth who were unable to contribute, but gave us hope and encouragement and to our editorial goddess and print guru Patty Groff. Thanks to those who helped in every small way, our friends and family for their support and those who we may have forgotten.

Many thanks to our chefs Wayne Wipp and Tim Smyth for their culinary insight and for supplying additional recipes.

Extra special thanks to Tom Weaver for his steadfast advice and help with research and May Isaac for tireless help on the recipes and manuscript.

We'd like to give a warm thank you to all our contributors for taking the time to contribute something to our special project.

Geoff Isaac
Gordon Reid

This book is dedicated to the memory of:

Robert C. Isaac

Clarence and Shirley Reid

BREAKFASTS

"IT'S BREAKFAST TIME."

· BIG BRAIN (DESMOND ASKEW)

THE HILLS HAVE EYES (2006)

JUNE WILKINSON'S
ITALIAN EGGS

Born in Essex, England, the voluptuous Wilkinson, made a name for herself on the cover of Playboy and eventually won film roles. She did theatre and appeared in nightclubs working with Spike Jones who admired her comedic talents. She eventually went on to film work and received a role in *Batman* as the villainess Evelina. She now runs fitness clubs in Canada from her home in California.

INGREDIENTS

¼ pound butter	Oregano
1 large tomato	1 sprig parsley
4 eggs	Salt and pepper
4 ounces (½ cup) Cheddar cheese	Brown bread slices

DIRECTIONS

Melt butter in a skillet to coat the bottom well. Place tomato, sliced in six pieces, in the skillet on low heat, cover, and fry on one side for about 2 minutes. Toss in salt and pepper to taste, cover and fry tomatoes on other side for 2 minutes. Remove tomatoes and set aside.

Crack the eggs and evenly distribute in skillet. Cover the eggs evenly with chopped hunks of Cheddar cheese and add salt and pepper to taste. Sprinkle lightly with oregano and fresh, chopped parsley. Cover skillet and cook on low heat for about 5 minutes.

Toast bread and butter it lightly. Place tomatoes on bread. When eggs are done, remove from pan with a spatula and place on your buttered toast. Sprinkle with additional parsley for decoration and serve with fruit on the side.

Serves: 2

YVETTE VICKERS'S
ZUCCHINI, ONION AND CHEESE FRITTATA

Born in Kansas City, Missouri, Vickers majored in theater at UCLA appeared in James Cagney's directorial debut as well as *Hud* and *What's the Matter With Helen?* She is best known to cult B-movie fans for her work in *Attack of the Giant Leeches* and *Attack of the 50 Foot Woman*. Vickers was in a television episode of *One Step Beyond* and most recently appeared in *Evil Spirits*.

INGREDIENTS

1	tablespoon olive oil	4	eggs, beaten
1	garlic clove, minced		Salt and pepper
1	onion, chopped	1	cup Jalapeno Jack cheese, shredded
1	zucchini, chopped into small pieces		

DIRECTIONS

In medium hot fry pan, add the olive oil, fresh garlic, and onion. When onion is half done add the zucchini. When crunchy to taste, add the eggs, salt and pepper. Use a spatula to lift the eggs to help set the egg mixture. Now add the cheese on top. Cover 5 minutes. Enjoy with sourdough toast or bread of choice.

Serves: 2

SELECTED GENRE FILMOGRAPHY

YVETTE VICKERS (1936-)

TV:

One Step Beyond (1959)

FEATURES:

Attack of the 50 Foot Woman (1958)

Attack of the Giant Leeches (1959)

What's the Matter With Helen? (1971)

The Dead Don't Die (1975)

Evil Spirits (1990)

TASTY TITLES

Attack of the Killer Tomatoes! (1978)	*Flesh Eating Mothers (1989)*
Attack of the Mushroom People (1963)	*Late for Dinner (1991)*
Bad Taste (1987)	*Lunch Meat (1987)*
Blood Diner (1987)	*Munchies (1987)*
Blood Feast 2: All U Can Eat (2002)	*Naked Lunch (1991)*
Cannibal: The Musical (1996)	*Poultrygeist: Attack of the Chicken Zombies! (2006)*
Dead and Breakfast (2005)	*Pumpkinhead (1989)*
Eaten Alive: A Tasteful Revenge (1999)	*Top of the Food Chain (1999)*
	Trick or Treat (1986)
	Voodoo Soup (1994)

> **"WELL, ONE THING FOR SURE, YOU WON'T HAVE TO WORRY ABOUT FOOD, BECAUSE YOU FOLKS CAN EAT UP HERE A WHOLE YEAR AND NEVER HAVE THE SAME MENU TWICE."**
>
> **- HALLORANN (SCATMAN CROTHERS)**
>
> ***THE SHINING (1980)***

DAVID DUNCAN'S
EGGS DUNCAN

Duncan began as a science fiction novelist and went on to write cult B-horror titles before penning the critically acclaimed *The Time Machine*. Duncan continued to write for many television shows including the original *The Outer Limits* and *Daniel Boone* until the 1980's.

In a saucepan place 3 extra large eggs (unbroken) and the glass or mug that is to be their receptacle. Into the glass put a chunk of blue cheese. Any blue cheese or brie or limburger will do. Cheddar won't work. Add a large dollop of butter or margarine and a shot of half and half cream. I never measure anything.

Turn the heat on. I have an electric stove so I turn it high at first and turn it to low when the water gets warm. Do NOT let the water boil yet. Although I have a cooking thermometer, I never use it, but judge the temperature by putting a finger in the water and counting seconds: "Alligator one, alligator two etc…" If I jerk my finger out before getting to two, the water is too hot. If I can keep it there until I get to "alligator three," it's too cold.

After a few minutes of this, take an egg out, break it and dump it into the glass. By this time the cheese, butter and half and half in the glass should be thoroughly mixed and, if one has remembered, salt and pepper have been added.

Break and dump the second egg in and then the third. Turn the heat on high and stir the eggs continuously until the water boils. Lift the glass gingerly onto a plate or saucer. When the eggs are cool enough, drink them.

I usually have slices of French bread heavily smeared with a garlic spread and toasted along with the eggs. The garlic spread is merely soft margarine mixed with four or five cloves of finely diced garlic and enough paprika to give it a pink color. Such toast dunked in the eggs is very good.

"IF YOU CLOSE YOUR EYES, IT ALMOST FEELS LIKE YOU'RE EATING RUNNY EGGS."

- MOUSE (MATT DORAN) TO NEO (KEANNU REEVES) ON THEIR UNAPPEALING FOOD.

THE MATRIX (1999)

JIM DANFORTH'S
NO-CHOLESTEROL OMELET FOR BUSY PEOPLE

Danforth, a special-effects master, cut his creative teeth on films like *The Wonderful World of the Brothers Grimm* and *Jack the Giant Killer*, before continuing on the original *Outer Limits* television show. He was nominated for an oscar for his work on *7 Faces of Dr. Lao*. Danforth went on to visual effects work in *When Dinosaurs Ruled the Earth*, *Twilight Zone: The Movie* and *The Stuff* among many others. Danforth continues to work freelance in California.

INGREDIENTS

1	cup eggbeaters or other no-cholesterol egg substitute	1½	tablespoons dehydrated onion flakes
¼	teaspoon salt	⅓	cup water
½	tablespoon parsley flakes	¼	teaspoon canola oil

DIRECTIONS

Pour the canola oil into an electric skillet and spread with a spatula. Begin heating the skillet to 275° F.

Combine the remaining ingredients and stir briskly with a whisk until frothy.

Pour the frothy batter into the warming skillet and scrape the bottom of the skillet continually with a spatula, pushing and folding the batter toward the center.

After approximately one minute, the batter should have cooked to the point where it will remain mounded in the center of the skillet. Cover the skillet and cook for about eight minutes. The omelet should now be firm enough to be removed intact from the skillet. Top with Salsa or Marinara sauce.

Note: before eating the omelet, fill the skillet with water and scrape the sides and bottom with a spatula. This will make the later washing up much faster.

SELECTED GENRE FILMOGRAPHY

JIM DANFORTH

(Visual effects or animation)

TV:

The Outer Limits (1963)

Star Trek: The Cage (1966): (prop-maker)

FEATURES:

Assistant animator:
The Time Machine (1960) (uncredited)

Atlantis, the Lost Continent (1961)

Jack the Giant Killer (1962)

Journey To the Seventh Planet (1962)

Flight of the Lost Balloon (1962) (puppeteer)

When Dinosaurs Ruled the Earth (1970)

The Day Time Ended (1980)

Caveman (1981)

The Aftermath (1982)

The Thing (1982)

The Stuff (1985)

Day of the Dead (1985)

They Live (1988)

Body Snatchers (1993)

Body Bags (1993)

Dragonworld (1994)

The Prophecy (1995)

JACK CARTER'S
GARBAGE OMELET

INGREDIENTS

4	eggs	2	bacon strips
Milk		Spinach	
1	onion, sliced	Sour cream	
		Tomatoes	

DIRECTIONS

Mix the eggs with a bit of milk. Brown your onions first, then fold into egg mixture and add to the pan. While still moist and hot, fold in chopped tomatoes, bacon strips and spinach. Fold over to brown outside like a football. Top with sour cream and eat it yourself with scooped out bagels, toasted and filled with cream cheese.

BAD EGGS

Eggs. High in protein and nutritious but not all make for gourmet fare. Here is a short list of movies and their eggs to avoid:

Movie:	Egg becomes...
Alien (1979)	A face hugging concentrated acid for blood spewing alien.
Slither (2006)	A giant mind controlling slug
Critters (1986)	Small furry things with big teeth
Jurassic Park (1993)	Velociraptor dinosaur
Harry Potter and the Philosopher's Stone (2001)	Hagrid's pet dragon Norbert who singes his beard
The Monster That Challenged the World (1957)	Giant killer escargot discovered in the depths of the sea
Mothra (1961)	Giant killer Moth fights godzilla
Queen of Blood (1966)	Blood eating Alien
Willy Wonka and the Chocolate Factory (1974)	The spoiled Veruca Salt declared bad by an egg-sorting machine.

P.J. SOLES'S FAVORITE
BANANA PANCAKES

P.J. Soles made memorable appearances in the landmark horror films *Carrie* and *Halloween*. Soles, who was married to actor Dennis Quaid, went on to a starring role in the Ramones feature *Rock 'n' Roll High School*. This was followed by the army comedies *Private Benjamin* and *Stripes*.

INGREDIENTS

1	cup milk	2	teaspoons baking powder
1	egg		Pinch of salt
3	tablespoons butter, melted		
¾	cup all-purpose flour	1	small ripe banana
2	tablespoons sugar	¼	cup chopped pecans or walnuts (optional)

DIRECTIONS

Whisk together eggs and milk and add melted butter. Sift the dry ingredients and mix in a separate bowl. Gradually add egg mixture to dry ingredients, stirring until just combined. Mash the banana with a fork and stir into the mixture along with the nuts.

Butter a large skillet and heat until a drop of water evaporates on contact. Pour out about ¼ cup of the batter and cook until bubbly and dry around the edges. Turn pancakes over and cook for about a minute.

Serve sprinkled with raw cane sugar.

Makes: 10 4-inch pancakes.

BACK STORY

I was born in Germany, but raised in Morocco, Venezuela, and Belgium, so I was exposed to exotic foods, which I love. I love mangoes, tandoori chicken, curries, croissants, brie cheese, cherries, Moroccan lemon chicken, Key lime pie, crab cakes, seafood gumbo, and banana pancakes. I had banana pancakes in Jamaica — they were so delicious served on a wooden plate with raw cane sugar sprinkled over top — now it's one of my favorite breakfasts.

I make a killer gumbo, but I do not use bacon. I just use lots of fresh crab, oysters, shrimp, crawfish, clams, pieces of salmon, tuna, and swordfish. If I wasn't an actress, I would love to be a chef! I would love to go to the Culinary Institute in New York. by Hyde Park. That is my fantasy!

SELECTED GENRE FILMOGRAPHY

P.J. SOLES (1950-)

FEATURES:

Blood Bath (1976)

Carrie (1976)

The Possessed (1977)

Halloween (1978)

Innocent Prey (1984)

B.O.R.N. (1988)

Alienator (1989)

Out There (1995)

Mirror, Mirror IV: Reflection (2000)

Mil Mascaras vs. the Aztec Mummy (2005)

The Devil's Rejects (2005)

Death By Engagement (2005)

The Tooth Fairy (2006)

**"AREN'T THEY
LOVELY? WE CAN
HAVE THEM FOR
BREAKFAST."**

- MRS. OGRE
(KATHERINE HELMUND)
TIME BANDITS (1981)

DAVID MANNERS'S
SMOOTHIE

Manners was born in Halifax, Nova Scotia and was the leading man in three important horror films: *Dracula* (1931) opposite Bela Lugosi, *The Black Cat* and *The Mummy* opposite Boris Karloff. Manners then took the unusual step of leaving hollywood in 1936 for the theatre. He wrote spiritual books later on in life and still kept in touch with many of his leading ladies from the thirties including Katherine Hepburn.

This recipe comes from his caregiver. If you are not able to find Life Mix, try substituting a protein powder from your local health food store.

INGREDIENTS

2	tablespoons Life Mix	½	banana
6	ounces carrot juice		

DIRECTIONS

Put in blender and mix until smooth.

DAVID'S EGG

During the time David was with us, his most favorite meal was breakfast. He enjoyed his morning egg fried in butter and sunny side up. He would eat the white first, turning it very carefully so as not to break the yolk. Once in awhile, I would hear him groan, "Oh, I've fractured it." You see, he liked to plop the yolk into his mouth intact. It was like a game with him.

He enjoyed old fashioned desserts like custard, rice pudding, bread pudding and tapioca — food that was easy to eat and especially sweets.

**"THIS IS YOUR BRAIN ON THE
BOX. THIS IS MY BRAIN ON
THE BOX. DOES ANYBODY ELSE
FEEL LIKE A FRIED EGG?"**

- THE RIDDLER (JIM CARREY)
BATMAN FOREVER (1995)

BILLY GRAY'S SET FOOD
GRILLED BACON AND EGG SANDWICH

OUR PICK

Gray was a successful child actor who is best remembered as Bobby Benson in *The Day the Earth Stood Still* and James 'Bud' Anderson, Jr. in the popular fifties television show *Father Knows Best*. Gray's genre television work included *Alfred Hitchcock Presents* and his later films were *The Navy vs. the Night Monsters* and *Werewolves on Wheels*. Gray is a bike racing enthusiast and resides in California.

INGREDIENTS

2-3	slices of bacon cut in half	Salt and pepper
1	egg	2 slices of your favorite bread, buttered on one side

DIRECTIONS

Cook bacon in skillet. Pour off the fat and drain the bacon on a paper towel. Place one slice of bread butter side down in the skillet. Arrange bacon on top. Break an egg over it. Sprinkle with salt and pepper. Add second slice of bread butter side up. Press down with a spatula and cook until golden on both sides. Some of the egg will escape out of the sides of the sandwich but that's the nature of a bacon and egg sandwich.

Serves: 1

ON THE SET...

My favorite "show biz" food is the sandwich that was always available on short notice from the "Lunch Wagon" when you first showed up for work. I got calls in the 7am to 8am range. The crew was normally there an hour or so earlier. So the grill was hot and the only trouble was getting the cooks' attention. The sandwiches were really good with the bread grilled like a cheese sandwich. It had an egg, yolk broken with two strips of bacon. Soft and warm and delicious.

SELECTED GENRE FILMOGRAPHY

BILLY GRAY (1938-)

www.billygray.com

TV:

The Adventures of Superman (1952)

Alfred Hitchcock Presents (1955)

FEATURES:

Abbott and Costello Meet the Killer, Boris Karloff (1949)

The Day the Earth Stood Still (1951)

The Navy vs. the Night Monsters (1966)

Werewolves on Wheels (1971)

EVELYN ANKERS AND RICHARD DENNING
TUTU'S OATMEAL

Richard Denning began his career in Hollywood in the 1930's after winning a screen test from a radio contest. He is best remembered by fans for his work in *Creature from the Black Lagoon, Target Earth* and *Creature With the Atom Brain*. Denning married the Universal Films Evelyn Ankers. Denning's last fantasy film was *Twice-Told Tales* with Vincent Price.

The stunning Evelyn Ankers was born in Chile to British parents. After small roles in British films, she emigrated to the United States. Horror fans immediately recall her horrified screams in the clutches of *The Wolf Man* with Lon Chaney Jr. Ankers went on to fame in many Universal chillers including *The Mad Ghoul*, *Son of Dracula* and *The Invisible Man's Revenge*. Ankers married Richard Denning in 1942 and retired from films and television in the early 1960's.

INGREDIENTS

4 cups water or milk, boiled (can be mixed 50/50)	1 cup plain bran flakes
¼ teaspoon salt, optional	¼ cup brown sugar
2 cups oats	½ grated coconut
	¼ cup chunky peanut butter

DIRECTIONS

Combine all ingredients.

To cook the oatmeal, boil the water and milk. Add the rest of the ingredients while slowly stirring. After all ingredients are thoroughly mixed, cover and turn down to simmer for 5 to 10 minutes on low, stirring occasionally.

Yummy and healthy!

Serves: 4

Photo: Evelyn Denning and Richard Denning with daughter Dee Ankers Denning.

OATMEAL TRIVIA

To create the sound of the T-1000 morphing into various shapes in *Terminator 2: Judgement Day*, sound effects technicians put a condom over a microphone and dipped it in oatmeal.

The special effects crew used 250 gallons of oatmeal to create the giant Spinosaur droppings in *Jurassic Park III*.

For a volcano scene in *The Time Machine (1960)*, oatmeal with orange and red food coloring was used to simulate the lava.

OOPS! In a memorable scene in Peter Jackson's *Dead Alive*, the film's hero Lionel is serving zombies porridge. He feeds a nurse zombie tranquilized porridge which she swallows only to have it pour out her throat. After he pours more into her throat, the porridge disappears.

BRUCE CAMPBELL'S
FAVORITE BREAKFAST

Birmingham, Michigan born Bruce Cambpell broke through with longtime friend Sam Raimi when the two made the landmark slasher *The Evil Dead* with Campbell starring as "Ash." He has since gone on to become a beloved genre icon. Mainstream audiences know him best as the ruthless Coach Boomer in *Sky High* and an equally unforgiving usher in Raimi's *Spiderman II*. He is author of the novel *Make Love! The Bruce Campbell Way* and his autobiography *If Chins Could Kill: Confessions of a B Movie Actor.*

Hot Grape Nuts with a touch of cinnamon, honey and rice milk. Can't beat it for the days when you've got to hack up some "deadites!"

SELECTED GENRE FILMOGRAPHY

BRUCE CAMPBELL (1958-)

FEATURES:

The Evil Dead (1981)

Evil Dead II (1987)

Maniac Cop (1988)

Darkman (1990)

Army of Darkness (1993)

Escape From L.A. (1996)

From Dusk Till Dawn 2: Texas Blood Money (1999)

Spider-Man (2002)

Bubba Ho-tep (2002)

Spider-Man 2 (2004)

Man With the Screaming Brain (2005)

Bubba Nosferatu (2006)

"IT WORKED JACK. YOU JUST DIGESTED THE BAD GUY."

- TEMPLETON PUCK (DENNIS QUAID)
INNERSPACE (1987)

CLAUDE RAINS
SCRAMBLED EGGS WITH TRUFFLES AND KIPPERS

OUR PICK

Born in London, England, Rains came to the United States after teaching and acting on the stage in England. Rains is best remembered by movie lovers for the classic title role in *The Invisible Man (1933)* and his roles in *Casablanca* and *Notorious*. Rains went on to appear in *Here Comes Mr. Jordan*, *The Wolf Man*, *Phantom of the Opera* and *The Lost World* as well as many *Alfred Hitchcock Presents* television episodes.

INGREDIENTS

4	kippers, cooked	½	teaspoon truffles or
1	tablespoon butter	2	tablespoons truffle oil
4	eggs		Parsley
¼	cup cream		Salt and pepper
			Whole wheat toast

DIRECTIONS

In a small bowl, add cream to eggs and mix with a fork. Add butter to a pan on medium heat and scramble the eggs until cooked but not dry. Add truffles, and stir to combine. Serve on toast with kippers.

Serve with a glass of champagne and orange juice.

"EGGIWEGS! I WOULD LIKE TO SMASH THEM!"
- ALEX (MALCOLM MCDOWELL)
A CLOCKWORK ORANGE (1971)

"I'LL BE IN HELL FOR BREAKFAST."
- TINKER (JOE UNGER)
TEXAS CHAINSAW MASSACRE III (1990)

ALIEN BREAKFAST QUICHE

INGREDIENTS

2	sheets of puff pastry	6	strips of roasted red pepper, chopped fine
4	shallots	½	cup of prosciutto, shredded
1¼	cup Gruyere cheese, grated	6	eggs
¾	cup Swiss cheese, grated	2	egg yolks
8	stalks of asparagus, chopped into ¼ inch pieces	2	cups heavy cream
			Salt and white pepper

DIRECTIONS

Place a sheet of pastry in a 9-inch spring form pan and press down firmly at sides and bottom. Place the second sheet on a 90 degree angle to the first and press pastry against sides of the pan. The corners of the pastry will stick up.

Saute the asparagus on medium heat until soft, remove from pan and set aside. Add the shallots, and red pepper and saute until soft.

Add half the cheese to the bottom of the pastry lined spring form.

Sprinkle the vegetables and prosciutto over the cheese and add the rest of the cheese on top.

Beat the eggs, cream, salt and pepper, and pour over top. Place strips of aluminum foil around edges of pastry to prevent burning.

Bake in 350°F for 80 to 90 minutes or until top is firm.

Serve with cappuccino.

Serves: 4

"ALL I WANTED WAS A LITTLE ORDER. A SLICE OF QUICHE WOULD BE NICE."

-GENERAL DELATOMBE'S (JONATHAN PRYCE) LAST WORDS.

THE BROTHERS GRIMM, THE (2005)

DANA WYNTER'S
BANANA SANDWICH

Born in Berlin, Germany, fans know Wynter best for her portrayal of Becky Driscoll in *Invasion of the Body Snatchers (1956)*. Wynter has appeared in well over 50 television shows, including one of Alfred Hitchcock's favorite one hour episodes of his own *The Alfred Hitchcock Hour*, entitled "An Unlocked Window." Wynter is now a journalist and animal rights activist.

I'm a poor choice because I don't care one way or another about food. I was a child during World War II, the cooking was dreadful in our house and my father was a doctor, so mercifully there were never set meals.

Here's my contribution:

Take one banana, slice or mash it. Butter two slices of fresh bread; place the banana between them. Sugar or shaved chocolate could be a good substitute for the banana.

The Actress, the Car, the Blond and her Avacado

I was traveling in a car in South Africa with a blonde friend sitting behind me. The astonished glances from Africans we passed led me to look in the rear-view mirror to find she'd eaten half her avocado and spread the other half on her face. "Does the skin good" she said.

"WOULD YOU CARE TO SHARE MY TOASTED CHEESE SANDWICH?"
- NORMAN BATES
PSYCHO III

"I'LL BLOW THIS PLACE UP AND BE HOME IN TIME FOR CORN FLAKES!"
- COHAAGEN (RICHARD)
TOTAL RECALL (1990)

LARRY COHEN
...ON MOVIE FOOD

Writer, producer and director Larry Cohen, born in New York City, wrote early TV genre shows like *Way Out*. Cohen created and wrote *The Invaders* television show and went on to direct cult favorites *It's Alive*, *The Stuff*, *Q*, *Maniac Cop* and a *Masters of Horror* television episode, "Pick Me Up" (2006).

Since the actors in *The Stuff* had to eat huge amounts of the goop, we used whipped cream and the cast kept getting fatter from scene to scene. For the huge amounts of it we used fire-fighting foam that's made up out of ground fish bones. You can imagine the smell of it. After one scene in upstate New York, the actors and stuntmen simply jumped into the Hudson River because they couldn't stand it any more. Imagine the desperation that'd make anyone jump into the Hudson River which is not known for it's cleanliness.

In my film *It's Alive* we needed huge amounts of milk to pour out of the back of a milk truck (whose driver had been murdered by the Mondtor baby). We mixed powdered milk into large Sparklett's water bottles and poured it out of the truck and mixed it with stage blood.

On my film *Bone* we needed a dead rat which our hair designer provided and dyed black. When I asked him where he'd put it, he told me he'd left it in my refrigerator. I freaked! A dead rat in there in my home — in my fridge. I had everything in it thrown out, but it was worth it for the laughs the crew got out of it. That's what you get for filming in your own house.

Feeding the crew is always a hassle and like an army unit they complain about the food endlessly. Finally, my ex-wife Janelle couldn't stand the bitching over the food so she cooked a gourmet dinner for the entire crew. Six courses of it. And they complained about it! After that she told me, "Feed them whatever you want!"

The moral: You can't please the crew, just make the movie!

SELECTED GENRE FILMOGRAPHY

LARRY COHEN
(1938-)

TV:

Writer:
Way Out (1961)

Creator:
The Invaders (1967)

Writer:
The Invaders (1995)

Director:
Masters of Horror (2006)

FEATURES:

Writer:
Scream, Baby, Scream (1969)

Director:
It's Alive (1974)

God Told Me To (1976)

It Lives Again (1978)

Full Moon High (1981)

Q, the Winged Serpent (1982)

Special Effects (1984)

The Stuff (1985)

It's Alive III: Island of the Alive (1987)

A Return To Salem's Lot (1987)

Wicked Stepmother (1989)

The Ambulance (1990)

Writer:
Maniac Cop (1988)

Badge of Silence (1993)

Body Snatchers (1993)

COLEEN GRAY'S
GLORIOUSLY GRITTY CORNBREAD

Nebraska born Gray began work in Hollywood in the 1940's, with roles in classic noirs *The Kiss of Death* and *Nightmare Alley*. She had a starring role in *The Leech Woman* and also starred in *The Vampire* and *The Phantom Planet*. She guest starred in numerous soap operas and weekly television shows during the sixties and seventies.

INGREDIENTS

1 cup corn meal	1 teaspoon baking powder
½ cup Fearn's Corn Germ (found in health food stores)	¼ teaspoon salt
	¼ teaspoon baking soda
¼ cup oat bran	¾ cup sour milk
¼ cup protein powder	1 egg
2 tablespoons raw sugar	1 tablespoon vegetable oil or melted butter

DIRECTIONS

Sift dry ingredients. Add and stir in the milk, egg, and oil.

If mixture is too thick, add a tad more sour milk. If too thin, add more corn meal. Spray a 6x10 Pyrex or stainless steel loaf pan with cooking spray. Pour in the mixture. Bake in 350°F pre-heated oven for 30 minutes, or until it passes the toothpick test and shrinks slightly from the sides. Serve with honey and butter.

"HERE'S SOME CORNBREAD."

- RIPLEY (SIGOURNEY WEAVER) TO PARKER (YAPHET KOTTO).

ALIEN (1979)

" I GUESS SHE DON'T LIKE THE CORNBREAD, EITHER."

- FROST (RICCO ROSS) UPON SEEING RIPLEY SMACK THE BREAKFAST TRAY AWAY.

ALIENS (1986)

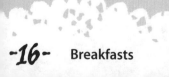

ROBERT SAWYER
...ON THE FUTURE OF FOOD

Ottawa born Sawyer has won 38 national and international awards for his fiction, including the 1995 Nebula Award for his novel *The Terminal Experiment*. Sawyer, a science-fiction writer and educator was dubbed the dean of Canadian science fiction by the Ottawa Citizen in 1999. In 2003 Sawyer won a Hugo Award for his novel *Hominids*. Sawyer continues to write from his home in Mississauga, Ontario.

We had to wonder what food would be like in the future. For the answer we asked futurist and award winning science fiction author Robert Sawyer.

Food is one of humanity's great pleasures, and in the future, it's only going to get better. Instead of changing foods, genetic engineering will change us, and the way we digest.

Why should the foods we like best be the least good for us? Future generations of humanity will be able to eat any food, no matter how rich. Sugar, salt, fat, cholesterol — all the things we love but have to consume in moderation now will have no restrictions on them in the future. All food will be nutritious; the sole criterion for choosing meals will be taste.

And, of course, dishes that haven't been enjoyed for thousands of years will be back on the menu: we will resurrect mammoths and moas from recovered DNA. *Jetsons*-style food pills will never materialize; instead, in the future, enjoying sumptuous meals will be a guilt-free highlight of every day.

"WE'VE HAD ONE, YES. WHAT ABOUT SECOND BREAKFAST?"
- PIPPEN (BILLY BOYD)
LORD OF THE RINGS: FELLOWSHIP OF THE RING (2001)

MEMORABLE BREAKFASTS

It's the most important meal of the day. We've listed the best of the best. Here are some of the most memorable breakfasts:

OVERABUNDANCE OF BREAKFAST

Pleasantville (1998)	Reese Witherspoon's breakfast is huge! Blueberry pancakes, scrambled eggs, sausage, crisp bacon, a ham steak. The table is piled high with tea biscuits and waffles.
Hellboy (2004)	Hellboy's favorite meal consists of gargantuan bowls of pancakes and ham in Guillermo del Toro's adaptation of the Mike Mignola comic books.
Caveman (1981)	A pterodactyl egg becomes a giant omelet for cavemen in Carl Gottlieb's comedy-fantasy starring Ringo Starr.

MORE TRADITIONAL FARE

An American Werewolf in London (1981)	Bacon and eggs, porridge, orange juice and toast with jam is on the menu for werewolf victim David Kessler (David Naughton) when he wakes up in the hospital.
War of the Worlds (1953)	An idyllic eggs, toast and coffee breakfast until a flying saucer crashes and ruins it.
V for Vendetta (2005)	Evey (Natalie Portman) wakes up to fried toast with egg in the middle prepared by V (Hugo Weaving).
Being John Malkovich (1999)	Toast and coffee with the morning paper is seen by Craig Schwartz (John Cusack) through the eyes of actor John Malkovich.
The 'burbs	In breakfast scene a character is eating breakfast and a box of Gremlins cereal is on the kitchen counter behind him. The director of The Burb's, Joe Dante, also directed Gremlins (1984).
Incredible Shrinking Man (1957)	One egg with orange juice pre-shrinking.

SOMETHING DIFFERENT

Star Wars (1977)	Aunt Beru prepares breakfast with a green vegetable similar to husked corn.
White Noise (2005)	Michael Keaton spoons fruit salad into a bowl in the opening scene.
The Matrix (1999)	"A single-celled protein combined with synthetic aminos, vitamins and minerals."
Hitch-hikers guide to the Galaxy (2005)	Burnt Toast, peanuts and beer moments before the world is destroyed by an alien race making room for an inter-galactic highway.

AUTOMATIC BREAKFASTS

Big Fish (2003)	Young Ed Bloom (Ewan McGregor) wins a science fair with his breakfast machine.
Edward Scissorhands (1990)	A Pancake making machine invented by Vincent Price is both a pre-Edward invention and inspiration.
Chitty Chitty Bang Bang (1968)	Breakfast machine makes bread, fried egg and sausage.
Gremlins (1984)	An overzealous automatic egg cracker and orange juicer are standard creations for inventor and Mogwai customer Randall Peltzer (Hoyt Axton).

FOR STARTERS

ARTHUR HILLER
GWEN HILLER'S "LAZY" CHEESE KNISHES

Arthur Hiller graduated from the Victoria School for the Performing and Visual Arts in his birthplace of Edmonton, Alberta. He directed the very first episode of *The Addams Family* TV show. Hiller also directed numerous episodes of *Alfred Hitchcock Presents* and *Thriller* with Boris Karloff as host. Box office success came with *Love Story* and *Silver Streak*. Hiller was once president of the Directors Guild and a recipient of the Jean Hersholt Humanitarian Oscar and continues to work in California.

INGREDIENTS

DOUGH:

1	cup white flour
½	cup butter
1	cup cottage cheese, well drained

FILLING:

6	ounces cottage cheese, drained (or use farmer-style cheese)
1	egg

Pinch of salt

Sugar and cinnamon (if you desire a sweeter taste)

DIRECTIONS

Method for dough: Combine flour and butter. Toss it lightly with your fingers or use a pastry blender. Add cheese and combine. Chill overnight.

Method for filling: Combine cottage cheese, eggs and salt and sugar and cinnamon if used. Roll dough on floured board to a sheet about 1/8 inch thick. Cut out round shapes about 1½ inch in diameter, or triangular shapes of similar size. Place a small amount of cheese in center of each shape, dampen edge of dough with water and pinch dough together on all sides, enclosing cheese. Bake about 15 minutes at 425°F.

KNISHES TO THE RESCUE!

Thanksgiving came along while we were filming *Man Of La Mancha* in Rome so my dear wife, Gwen, decided she would cook a Thanksgiving dinner for all the Americans working with us. Well, have you tried to prepare an American Thanksgiving in Rome? Don't! Yams and cranberries are non-existent. Gwen finally convinced a greengrocer on the Via Del Croce to import them for her. It took a couple of weeks, but she got it all together and we had a great time. In addition to the American group we invited Sophia Loren and Peter O'Toole.

Mistake!

Neither of them could stand the sweet taste of yams or the cranberries. Fortunately, Gwen had some cheese knishes that she cooked earlier, in the refrigerator. She served them and Sophia and Peter were in heaven! They ate away at the knishes while the rest of us enjoyed our traditional Thanksgiving dinner.

> **"OH, GREAT THEN. SAVED BY NIBBLES."**
>
> - DAVID (DYLAN MORAN) ON THE ONLY FOOD AVAILABLE
>
> *SHAUN OF THE DEAD (2004)*

JIM DANFORTH
...ON THE WORST MARGARITA

I arrived in Durango Mexico to prepare for the filming of *Caveman* a few days before the actual shooting was scheduled to begin and checked into the hotel. One afternoon, with nothing to do, it occurred to me that here in Mexico, at a first class hotel, it should be possible to get a really fine margarita. To my surprise, this proved not to be the case. I don't know what ingredients the bartender was using, but it was the worse margarita I've ever had.

Later that day, in the lobby of the hotel, I encountered the physically imposing football star and actor John Matuszak (who would be playing the role of "Tonda" — the villain of *Caveman*).

"Want to join me in a pitcher of margaritas?" asked John.

"Bad idea, John," I replied. "They don't know how to make a margarita here."

"They do now," John said, "I just had a little talk with the bartender."

Apparently the bartender realized that arguing with "The Tooz" might be a bad idea; the margaritas were now first class. I wish I'd asked John what his recipe was.

CURTIS HARRINGTON'S
SHRIMP AND MUSHROOM STARTER

Los Angeles born Harrington, began his career making experimental films and was a protege of Roger Corman before directing the atmospheric *Night Tide* with Dennis Hopper. A friend of James Whale in his later years, Harrington coached Ian McKellen for Bill Condon's *God's and Monsters*.

I often entertain and always do the cooking for my friends. During his last years, I sometimes had Vincent Price and his wonderful actress wife, Coral Browne, come to dinner. I particularly remember how nervous I was preparing food for Vincent Price, since he was such a famous gourmet cook in his own right. Therefore, I was especially proud when Mrs. Price tucked in to the first course dish I served, which she referred to, in the British way, as a "starter." She tasted it, and said, "This is the best starter I've ever tasted." And here's the recipe:

INGREDIENTS

2	tablespoons butter	½	cup sour cream
1	tablespoons virgin olive oil		salt and pepper
3	green onions or shallots, chopped	2	tablespoons fresh parsley, chopped fine
½	pound mushrooms (fresh), sliced	2	tablespoons sherry (medium)
½	pound shrimp-shelled, deveined and pre-boiled	4	slices trimmed toast sautéed lightly in butter

DIRECTIONS

In a sauté pan cook onions in butter and oil for 2 minutes. Add mushrooms and shrimp and cook for 5 minutes. Season with salt and freshly ground black pepper to taste and stir in sour cream slowly. Heat thoroughly. Add sherry and parsley and serve on sautéed toast.

This is a simple but truly delicious recipe.

Nothing to me is more gratifying than the pleasure of cooking a good meal for friends and then sitting down with them to enjoy it together.

Serves: 4

HEALTH FOOD AND FRIENDS!

I have enjoyed the friendship of Robert Balzer, California's number one wine critic, for many years. I certainly consider wine to be an important element in any truly first rate meal.

When I made my television film, *Killer Bees*, starring Gloria Swanson, we shot the whole thing in Napa Valley, mostly in a house that since has become the private residence of Francis Coppola. Since Mr. Balzer was an old friend of Gloria's, I gave him a small part in the film. He had studied acting at RADA in London and he introduced us to some of the best wines of the region while we were there.

Gloria, of course, was a famous health food advocate, and one day Mr. Balzer told me that Gloria really liked me a lot. I thought he meant that she liked the way I was directing her until he mentioned, "She likes you because you brought your juicer here!" (I had brought my vegetable juicer with me to give me extra energy at work.) Suffice it to say, Gloria and I developed a great rapport together and remained good friends until her passing a few years later.

"YOU LOOK LIKE YOUR FACE FELL IN THE CHEESE DIP BACK IN 1957."
- NADA (RODDY PIPER)
THEY LIVE (1988)

"YEAH, BUT JOHN, IF THE PIRATES OF THE CARIBBEAN BREAKS DOWN, THE PIRATES DON'T EAT THE TOURISTS."
- IAN MALCOLM (JEFF GOLDBLUM)
JURASSIC PARK (1991)

FAVORITE DRINKS:

Guinness — room temp!

SUSAN AND JASON CARTER'S
GUACAMOLE SUPREME

Born in London and raised in Gainsborough, Carter studied at the London Academy of Music and Dramatic Art. His first role was as Hawkwing in the long running BBC television series *Jackanory* and had starring roles in plays in London's west end. Since moving to the United States, he appeared in numerous television shows until landing the role as Marcus Cole on *Babylon 5*. He lives in California with his wife Susan and children and has published poetry.

INGREDIENTS

3   ripe Hass avocados

2   scallions, diced

2   medium tomatoes, chopped

¼   cup chopped fresh cilantro

¼   cup sour cream

1   clove fresh garlic, chopped

Juice of half a lemon

Garlic salt

*Jalapeno peppers, (optional)

DIRECTIONS

Mash avocados, add rest of ingredients in order. Save an avocado pit to place in the dip to keep it from turning brown. Serve with warm tortilla chips and enjoy!

*but be careful.

"WELL, SHE SOUNDS LIKE A MEXICAN APPETIZER."

- FRANKLIN 'FOGGY' NELSON (JON FAVREAU) ON HEARING ELEKTRA NATCHIOS'S NAME.

DAREDEVIL (2003)

JESSICA RAINS'S
EASY HORS 'D'OEUVRES

Daughter of actor Claude Rains, Jessica appeared in Woody Allen's *Sleeper* and the TV horror film *Scream, Pretty Peggy*. She made several appearances in TV episodes before turning to producing low budget horror films like *Dead of Night* and *Psycho Cop*.

DIRECTIONS

Take the skin off of some Brie cheese.

Place pine nuts on a baking sheet and toast at 350°F for 8 minutes on the upper shelf.

Put the brie and one teaspoon of apricot jam in a bowl and melt in the microwave at medium for a minute.

Add the toasted pine nuts and serve with big chunks of bread.

MICHELLE NOLDEN'S
BRIE CHEESE AND PASTRY

Born in Brantford, Ontario, Michelle is best known to fans as T'than in *Earth: Final Conflict* and has made appearances on *Everwood*, *Crossing Jordan* and *CSI: Miami*. She continues to work in television and movies.

INGREDIENTS

1   package Pillsbury
    Crescent roll
Brie cheese

Dutch mustard
Sunflower seeds

DIRECTIONS

Roll out crescent dough, place brie in centre, spread with mustard and cover with seeds. Wrap up and cook at 325°F until pastry is cooked and golden brown.

Serve with crackers or fresh sourdough bread.

VERNON WELLS'S *MUSHROOMS DE STUFF*

Vernon Wells is usually found playing rugged often villainous roles in genre films. Among the best known is Mel Gibson's nemesis, the Mohawk sporting Wez in *Mad Max 2*; a role he later spoofed in John Hughes's *Weird Science*. He has demonstrated a talent for straight faced comedy as a well dressed hit man in Joe Dante's *Innerspace* and an Acme VP in *Back in Action*.

INGREDIENTS

3 or 4 medium sized mushrooms (portobello or shiitake)

1 teaspoon balsamic vinegar

3 tablespoons virgin olive oil

Ketchup

Honey

Heavy cream

DIRECTIONS

Wash and clean the mushrooms, leaving the stems. Heat a frying pan on low to medium heat, and carefully pour in virgin olive oil and balsamic vinegar.

Place mushrooms with the stem side up in a frying pan and gently pour a little ketchup, a little honey, and a little cream into the mushroom. Do not overfill! Salt and pepper to taste. Cook for approximately 4 to 6 minutes. And Voila!

Vernon's Mushrooms de stuff can be used as an appetizer or served with chicken, fish, or meat. If cooked too long, it will blacken and harden, and can then be used as a Christmas ornament.

"I DON'T WANT TO SERVE YOU APPETIZERS. I NEED YOU TO 'BE' APPETIZERS."

- FUAD RAMSES III
BLOOD FEAST 2: ALL U CAN EAT (2002)

KASEY ROGERS'S
SPECIAL OCCASION CHAMPAGNE PUNCH

Originally from Morehouse, Missouri, Rogers (aka Laura Elliott), was best known as Louise Tate on *Bewitched*. Rogers had a memorable turn as the doomed wife of Farley Granger in Alfred Hitchcock's *Strangers on a Train*. Rogers also wrote screenplays and books many based on *Bewitched* and kept active her entire life.

INGREDIENTS

1   bottle Dom Perignon champagne (optional)
2   bottles less expensive champagne (much less expensive)
1   large bottle of Sauterne

DIRECTIONS

Chill wine ahead of time when possible.

Set unopened bottle of Dom Perignon in front of punch bowl in full view of guests. This is just to impress them. Never waste Dom Perignon in a punch!

Mix together:

1   cup sugar
2   cups lemon juice (bottled juice is o.k.)
1   12-ounce can pineapple chunks, drained
1   large package frozen strawberries

Pour 2 bottles of champagne and 1 bottle Sauterne into punch bowl.

Add sugar, lemon juice, pineapple chunks and frozen strawberries to the wine in punch bowl and blend.

Add Giant Ice Cube (recipe follows.) Chill and serve.

It is highly suggested that you have plenty of refill ingredients handy. This is delicious and goes fast.

KASEY ROGERS'S
GIGANTIC ICE CUBE

INGREDIENTS

Water

Fresh strawberries
Pineapple chunks (if desired)

DIRECTIONS

Prepare a few days ahead. I always make 3 or 4.

Pour water into very large bowl or square container. Add fresh strawberries and pineapple. Freeze in advance.

Unmold and float in champagne punch.

For Halloween, instead of fresh fruit, I freeze large black plastic spiders and flies, strips of red bell pepper for blood and chunks of yellow papaya for... never mind. Be sure plastic critters are too large to swallow.

Use your imagination for different holidays.

PROP SWITCH

My favorite food story happened on the *Bewitched* set. First of all, everyone knows that you never really drink on a set, never in a scene, and never when working. The prop department will serve 7-Up, fruit juice or anything that looks like the real thing.

One evening, it was the last shot of the day and Stephane, the Tates and a client were having dinner, as usual, at Samantha's house. We were all seated around the dining room table.

The table was filled with delicious food (that's real), and grape juice filled our wine glasses.

Bill Asher, Liz's husband and our director, called "roll 'em," and the scene began. The conversation was lively, the food was yummy and one-by-one each of us took a sip of our "wine."

"I NEVER DRINK... WINE!"
- COUNT DRACULA (GARY OLDMAN)
DRACULA (1992)

Imagine our surprise when we found out we were sipping real wine. In fact, it was Sangria! As each individual discovered real wine filled our glasses, our eyes darted to Elizabeth.

She sat smiling at the head of the table with this devilishly sparkling look on her face. Liz loved to play practical jokes. She had switched the grape juice for the Sangria and was enjoying the fireworks.

To our professional credit, every actor completed the scene perfectly, never breaking character.

Bill yelled "Cut and print. That's a wrap."

We all burst out laughing, finished our glass of wine and went home.

Best witches,

Kasey Rogers.

BAD BREWS

What's a horror movie without a good potion or two? Here are some brews you may want to avoid:

Dr. Jekyll and Mr Hyde – The famous potion that turns Dr. Jekyll into Mr. Hyde in both the Lon Chaney silent and the Fredric March versions.

Street Trash (1987) – A liquor store owner discovers a new beverage which causes the drinker to melt.

Harry Potter and the Chamber of Secrets – The polyjuice potion. Changes you into whoever you want to be, but tastes really awful and only works on humans!

Cabin Fever (2002) – Water from a contaminated Lake turns people into diseased zombies. Next time bring bottled water.

Kwaidan – A haunted cup of tea is featured in the last segment of this Japanese horror classic.

The Nutty Professor (1963, 1996) – The potion that turns a nutty professor into Buddy Love.

The Princess Bride – Poisoned wine is the downfall of a character in this game of wits.

The Devil's Backbone – The fetal preservative or "limbo water" made with various spices, cloves and rum. Sold in town for medical purposes.

Eegah (1962) – A giant caveman (Richard Kiel) offers sulfur water that's kept him alive for eons to his modern guests.

TED BOHUS'S
BLOOD RED SANGRIA

Ted Bohus is editor and publisher of SPFX magazine and writes, directs and produces his own horror films.

INGREDIENTS

Half gallon of Red Vino (any old stuff will do)

1 cup orange juice

½ can of ginger ale

1 cup brandy

1 cup Triple Sec

1 whole orange, sliced

1 whole apple, sliced

DIRECTIONS

Stir and allow the flavors to blend for 30 minutes before adding ice and serving. For a stronger flavor, skip the ginger ale and add another ½ cup of brandy instead.

AUTHOR'S WARNING:

May be hazardous to your head the morning after.

BEST DRINKING SCENES

Raiders of the Lost Ark (1981) – Marion Ravenwood (Karen Allen) successfully drinks a local man under the table in this battle of the sexes drinking game and still manages to hand off a bottle of whisky to Indiana (Harrison Ford) to defeat the Nazis.

Clockwork Orange (1971) – Drinking milk at the Karova milk bar in the opening scene.

Forbidden Planet (1956) – Robby makes "rocket bourbon" for cook James Dirocco, (Earl Holliman) — 60 gallons worth in this loose science fiction adaptation of Shakespeare's ***The Tempest***.

Dr. Jekyll and Mr. Hyde (1931) – Dr. Jekyll creates the potion that splits his personality between good and bad.

The Shining (1980) – Jack Torrence at the bar having a drink with a long dead bartender.

Captain Kronos: Vampire Hunter (1974) – The first superhero vampire hunter film has Kronos (Horst Janson) defend his hunchback friend with a sharp sword against three bullies over the very best red wine.

Willy Wonka & the Chocolate Factory (1971) – Augustus Gloop drinks from a chocolate river with dire results.

The Lord of the Rings: The Return of the King (2003) – Dueling Elf (Legolas) and Dwarf (Gimli) attempt to out drink the other.

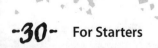

ALAN CAILLOU'S
FAVORITE DRINKS

Caillou (AKA Alan Lyle-Smythe) was an adventurer, who had served with the Palestinian Police in the 1930's and as a British Army Officer in the Intelligence Corp. Caillou went on to write for such television shows as *The Man from U.N.C.L.E.*, *The Six Million Dollar Man* and *Village of the Giants*. He also kept busy as a solid character actor and was last seen in *The Ice Pirates*.

Some recondite names you might not know, all well-known in certain locations:

Mother's Ruin: gin and tonic

Horse's Neck: gin and ginger ale

Alamagoozlum: (I kid you not!) — rum, chartreuse, white of egg (beaten), Angostura Bitters, cracked ice, water

Razor Blade: gin, lemon juice, cayenne pepper, cracked ice

Firing Squad: tequila, lime juice, grenadine, bitters, water

Angel's Kiss: marachino, cognac, heavy cream, ginger, nutmeg

Angel's Tit: maraschino, heavy cream, one scarlet cherry, strategically placed

All these are authentic; wander the world, you'll meet them sooner or later...

SELECTED GENRE FILMOGRAPHY

ALLAN CAILLOU (1914-2006)

TV:

Writer:
Thriller (1960)

Voyage to the Bottom of the Sea (1964)

The Man From U.N.C.L.E. (1964)

The Aquarians (1970)

Actor:
Thriller (1960)

The Man From U.N.C.L.E. (1964)

Quark (1977)

FEATURES:

Writer:
Village of the Giants (1965)

The Six Million Dollar Man: A Solid Gold Kidnapping (1973)

Kingdom of the Spiders (1977)

Actor:
Journey to the Center of the Earth (1959)

Five Weeks in a Balloon (1962)

Sole Survivor (1970)

The Questor Tapes (1974)

Herbie Goes to Monte Carlo (1977)

Beyond Evil (1980)

The Sword and the Sorcerer (1982)

The Ice Pirates (1984)

LEN BLUM'S
AFTER WORK-OUT PROTEIN SHAKE

Canadian screenwriter Len Blum went to the same school in Hamilton, Ontario as actor Eugene Levy. Blum, who co-wrote *Stripes* and *Meatballs* for director Ivan Reitman, got his start as a sound assistant for early Cronenberg films like *Rabid* and *Shivers*.

Slice a ripe banana and put in your blender.

Add four ice cubes, one scoop (28 g) of Chocolate Soy Protein Powder, available at your health food store, one tablespoon of light peanut butter, and two cups of skim milk.

Blend on low speed for a minute or so, until it sounds like the ice cubes have been crushed. Then blend on "high" for another minute or so to achieve that nostalgic "old-time milk-shake" consistency.

The only fat in this delicious drink is what's in the tablespoon of peanut butter.

Note: Adding more peanut butter does not make the shake taste any better. Nor does adding coffee, chocolate milk powder, chocolate syrup, or other fattening guck. The taste is perfect just as it is.

"WE SHALL DRINK TO OUR PARTNERSHIP. DO YOU LIKE GIN? IT IS MY ONLY WEAKNESS."
- DR. PRETORIUS (ERNEST THESIGER)
BRIDE OF FRANKENSTEIN (1935)

RICHARD MATHESON
MADRES

OUR PICK

Matheson has penned some of the most memorable and influential horror films, including *House of Usher, Pit and the Pendulum, Burn, Witch Burn!* and *The Devil Rides Out* among many others. Matheson's TV credits are no less impressive: *Alfred Hitchcock Presents, Thriller, The Twilight Zone* and the television film *Trilogy of Terror*. Matheson wrote the teleplay for Steven Spielberg's first feature length film, the chilling *Duel*. Matheson, also a noted novelist, continues to work in California.

INGREDIENTS

1½	ounces vodka	2	ounces cranberry juice
2	ounces orange juice	1	lime wedge (optional)

DIRECTIONS

Combine ingredients into a highball glass except lime and add ice. Add a squeeze of lime. Stir well. Serve with the wedge.

ANECDOTE

Many years ago, I wrote a story entitled F--- which, of course, usually means one thing but, in my story, meant Food which had become an obscene word due to the fact that all food had died out in the world and people presumably lived on chemical supplements; I don't know whether I went into that. The story is about a time traveler who goes into the future period of time. He has some small food items with him. After he is arrested for obscene behavior when the snacks are not only discovered in his time machine, but he repeats their names, not understanding why the police are in shock.

He is taken to the home of the Commissioner Castlemould who after drugging him with a "Vein Ball" collects the snacks together. When the time traveler regains consciousness, it is to see the Commissioner, face flushed with lust, eating the food while looking at "pornographic pictures" of various kinds of food, some of them held by leering women. The traveler manages to escape and get back to his machine and his own time. There he is congratulated for his feat and told that he is going to be taken out for a celebration steak dinner. The time traveler blushes.

LEAK AND STILTON TARTS

INGREDIENTS

20 3-inch pastry shells	2 tablespoons olive oil
2 leaks, diced, whites only	¼ cup of wine
½ cup heavy cream	1 tablespoon cornstarch
Salt and pepper	½ pound Stilton cheese, crumbled
Nutmeg	

DIRECTIONS

Pre-bake shells for 15 minutes. Follow package directions.

Sauté whites of leaks in the oil for 5 minutes or until soft.

Add the cream and wine and reduce heat to low. Add salt, pepper and nutmeg. Add the cornstarch to thicken and stir until quite thick.

Add mixture to the pastry shells.

Top with the Stilton in pieces to top of mix. Bake in oven for 15 minutes at 350°F.

Can be made ahead of time.

Serves: 8-10

CRAZY TRIVIA

Repo Man (1984) – All the food is labelled in the rather generic. "Beer", "Food" This is because the producers were unable to acquire any money for product placements from advertisers.

The Rocky Horror Picture Show (1975) – The wall of the laboratory includes chemical formulas and a grocery list for flour, eggs, bread, sugar and two hypodermics.

Lord of the Rings: Fellowship of the Ring (2001) – The catering department cooked and served 1,460 eggs to the cast and crew for breakfast during the entire shooting.

JOHN ZACHERLE
...*ON TV*

Known as "The Cool Ghoul" television host, Zacherle (aka Zacherley) had a hit record in 1958, entitled, "Dinner with Drac." Zacherle has edited horror anthologies and continues to make appearances in movies such as *Vampira: The Movie* as himself. Zacherle, who resides in New York, is a regular guest at the Chiller convention in New Jersey.

While toasting marshmallows on my Orgon machine (Tesla Coil) the spark would invariably shoot up the skewer and give me a wallop, a favorite part of the show for the fanatical viewers.

Making Dinosaur Egg Nog at special holiday seasons. The eggs are found in the swamps of New Jersey across from New York City in the area where the New York NFL teams now play football and where Jimmy Hoffa lies buried they say. The eggs are as big as watermelons. Crack them open and drop in a bunch of tenderized black widow spiders and let sit for a day or two — an unforgettable treat!

SELECTED GENRE FILMOGRAPHY

JOHN ZACHERLE aka Zacherley (1918-)

TV:

Horror Host: WPIX TV (New York City) as "The Cool Ghoul" (1963)

I Am Legend (Video) (1994) (as Himself)

Monsterama: A Tribute to Horror Hosts (2004)

FEATURES:

Geek Maggot Bingo (1983)

Horrible Horror (Video) (1986)

Frankenhooker (1990)

Niagaravation (1995)

Dr. Horror's Erotic House of Idiots (Video) (2003)

American Scary (2006)

Vampira: The Movie (2006)

FAVE FOODS:

Pan fried giant amoeba with twelve garlic cloves.

FAVE DRINK:

Dracula Fizz: One pint Swamp Water, ½ pound Bicarbonate of Soda. Drink fast in the presence of an EMS crew.

TAGLINES!

"IT BEGINS WITH THE MOST EVIL CRY, DEEP FROM THE TWISTED SHADOWS OF THE NIGHT. THEN, IT'S LAUGHTER LIKE SOME INSANE DOG RINGING IN YOUR EARS. IT COMES WITH THE JAWS OF HUNGRY HORROR - IT HUNGERS FOR YOU."

- SHOCK! SHOCK! SHOCK (1987)

"EVERYTHING IS ALIVE... AND HUNGRY."

- FROM BEYOND (1986)

DEVILED EGGS

INGREDIENTS

6 hard boiled eggs, halved   Mayonnaise
Curry powder   Mango chutney
Salt and pepper

DIRECTIONS

Remove yolks and pass through a sieve. To mayonnaise or
English salad dressing, add curry powder, salt and pepper.
Add to the egg yolks and mix thoroughly. Pile yolks in the
white halves. Top with a bit of mango chutney. Cover and
store in fridge until ready to use.

Makes: 12 deviled eggs

ASPARAGUS ROLLS

INGREDIENTS

White bread, slices   Salt and pepper
Asparagus, fresh   Butter
                             English salad cream
                             dressing or mayonnaise

DIRECTIONS

Steam asparagus until just tender. Remove from heat and
plunge into cold water and ice cubes. This maintains the
fresh green color and prevents overcooking. Place on
paper towels to dry and sprinkle with salt and pepper.

Slice bread very thinly and cut off crusts. Use a rolling pin
to gently flatten. The key is using very fresh bread. Butter
the bread lightly and spread with English salad dressing or
mayonnaise. Place one stalk of asparagus on each slice of
bread. Roll up tightly and place seam down in a cake pan.
Pack them closely together. Cover with plastic wrap and
store in the fridge until ready to use.

SMOKED SALMON SPIRALS

INGREDIENTS

Smoked salmon
thinly sliced

Chive cream cheese

Pepper, freshly ground

Romaine, centre
'vein' removed

Flour tortillas

DIRECTIONS

Spread tortillas with chive cream cheese. Top with salmon slices in a single layer. Sprinkle with pepper. Add a leaf of romaine lettuce. Roll up tortillas tightly and wrap each in plastic wrap. Place in a dish and store in the fridge. When ready to serve, unwrap and cut tortillas on the diagonal. The original recipe called for a crepe as the wrap, but this recipe is easier to make.

For a low-carb alternative, omit the tortillas. Spread each salmon slice with cream cheese and sprinkle with pepper. Use a romaine leaf as the wrap.

"SHAPE SHIFTING. WE DO IT FOR KICKS. TURN YOURSELF INTO A DIFFERENT ANIMAL. ONE NIGHT A DEER, NEXT NIGHT A SALMON."

- EDDIE HOLT (EDWARD JAMES OLMOS)
WOLFEN (1981)

"WOULD YOU CARE FOR AN HORS D'OEUVRE DOCTOR SEWARD? OR A CANAPE?"

- RENFIELD (TOM WAITTS) OFFERING FLIES TO DR SEWARD (RICHARD E. GRANTE).
BRAM STOKERS' DRACULA (1991)

LOBSTER DELIGHT

INGREDIENTS

¾	cup diced fennel	1	cup of fish stock
1	pound shelled lobster meat diced	1	cup heavy (35%) cream
		3	ounces of Pernod
2	tablespoons flour	3	ounces dry white wine
2	tablespoons butter	4	vol au vent pastries

DIRECTIONS

Simmer the cream, Pernod and wine for 3 minutes.

Add lobster and fish stock.

Saute fennel in butter until soft, then combine with lobster leaving butter in pan.

Add flour to butter to make a roux. Cook on low heat for 2 minutes, then whisk in the liquid.

Combine all ingredients and simmer 3 minutes more.

Place on top of the vol au vent pastry and serve.

Serves: 4

TAGLINES!

"FINALLY! THE ONLY MOTION PICTURE THAT DELIVERS SEAFOOD FROM OUTER SPACE!"
- *LOBSTER MAN FROM MARS (1989)*

"A MIND IS A TERRIBLE THING TO WASTE... ESPECIALLY IF YOU'RE REALLY HUNGRY"
- *THE RELIC (1997)*

SOUPS & SALADS

JAMES BERNARD'S
WATERCRESS SOUP

Son of a British Army Officer, Bernard was a college classmate of Christopher Lee. He then went on to be Hammer Films' most prolific film score composer.

INGREDIENTS

- 3 or 4 bunches of watercress
- 4 large potatoes
- 4 pints of chicken stock (if not home-made, stock cubes are perfectly okay)

DIRECTIONS

Note: This soup can be made the day before you need it, and kept in the fridge.

Peel potatoes and chop into quite small pieces (about ½ inch cubes or smaller) for quick cooking.

Bring chicken stock to the boil in large saucepan, add the chopped potatoes, bring back to the boil, then turn down heat and simmer gently (with lid on) for about 15 minutes, until the potatoes are soft.

While potatoes cook, wash watercress and remove bottom part of the stalks, which can be stringy. No need to chop the watercress further.

Add watercress to stock and potatoes, and allow mixture to boil gently for 1 minute only (2 minutes at most) This just softens the watercress, but retains the fresh taste and color. Allow to cool for a few minutes (or longer — it doesn't matter)

Put the mixture into electric blender and blend until it becomes smooth. Unless the container of the blender is extra large, you may have to do this in two or three portions, pouring each lot into a large bowl as you go along.

Add plenty of freshly ground black pepper and salt to taste, depending on the saltiness of the stock. You may like to add some cream or crème fraiche, but be careful, as this can detract from the pure watercress flavor.

When ready to serve the soup, simply reheat it in a large saucepan, but let it barely reach boiling point, or the flavor will become less fresh and the color a less intense green.

JEANNE BATES'S
CURRIED CELERY SOUP

Bates co-starred in numerous television shows including the memorable *Twilight Zone* episode, "It's a Good Life." She is also known to film buffs as Mrs. X in David Lynch's *Eraserhead* and memorable bits in *Die Hard 2* and *Mulholland Dr.*

INGREDIENTS

3	tablespoons butter or margarine	1½	teaspoon curry powder (I use more)
4	stocks of finely chopped celery	½	teaspoon salt
		¼	teaspoon pepper
3	tablespoons all-purpose flour	4	cups chicken broth
		2	cups milk

DIRECTIONS

Melt butter in 3 quart sauce pan over moderate heat. Add the celery and cook uncovered 5 minutes until tender-crisp.

Blend in flour and seasonings to make a paste.

Gradually stir in broth and milk. Puree in blender, and strain. Return to heat, stir consistently till it comes to a boil. Reduce heat, cover and simmer 10 minutes.

Serves: 6

My favorite cook was my husband.

"IS IT SOUP YET?"

– ALFREDO
LEATHERFACE: TEXAS CHAINSAW MASSACRE III (1990)

"I CAN'T STORM UP TO MY ROOM. I HAVEN'T HAD DIN-DIN"

- HERMAN (FRED GWYNN) TO LILY MUNSTER (YVONNE DE CARLO)
THE MUNSTERS (1964)

JEANNE BATES
(1918-)

TV:

One Step Beyond (1959)

The Twilight Zone (1961)

Wonder Woman (1978)

FEATURES:

The Phantom (1943)

The Return of the Vampire (1944)

Soul of a Monster (1944)

Back from the Dead (1957)

The Strangler (1964)

The Stranger (1973)

Topper Returns (1973)

Gus (1976)

Eraserhead (1977)

From the Dead of Night (1989)

Mom (1990)

Initiation: Silent Night, Deadly Night IV (1990)

JEFFREY COMBS'S
TORTILLA SOUP

California born and raised Jeffrey Combs did theatre after graduating from University of Seattle. It was his role as Herbert West in the critically acclaimed H.P. Lovecraft story *Re-Animator* that has made him a household name in the horror genre. Several roles in *Star Trek: Deep Space Nine* and every Star Trek series since have added to an already dedicated fan following.

INGREDIENTS

3	tablespoons canola oil
1	large yellow or red onion, chopped
1	large bell pepper, seeded and chopped
1	pound lean ground beef
2-3	jalapeno peppers, seeded and finely chopped
3-4	cloves of garlic, finely chopped
2	teaspoons chili powder
2	teaspoons ground cumin

2	28-ounce cans of ready cut tomatoes in puree
3	cups of water
2	15-ounce cans of pinto beans, drained and rinsed
½	cup fresh cilantro leaves, chopped
4	ounces light sour cream

Plain tortilla chips

Your favorite salsa

Salt

Pepper

DIRECTIONS

In a large skillet, heat the oil over medium heat. Add the onion, bell peppers and ground beef. Sauté until onions are translucent, approximately 5-10 minutes. Drain excess fat away. Add jalapenos, garlic, chili powder and cumin. Cook another 5 minutes on a slightly lower heat or until vegetables are tender. Be sure not to burn the garlic.

Transfer mixture to a large pot. Add tomatoes and water. Heat to boiling over high heat. Salt and pepper to taste. Reduce heat to low, cover and let simmer for 15 minutes. While simmering, chop the fresh cilantro.

Add beans and cook another 10 minutes.

After the soup is placed in individual bowls; top with a generous amount of cilantro, a dollop of sour cream, a touch of salsa and a handful of lightly crushed tortilla chips. Mix and enjoy.

Note: this soup always tastes better the next day. So, if you can, prepare it early, let it sit overnight in the fridge, heat it up and add toppings just before serving.

This soup makes a great first course, but it also makes a meal unto itself especially if served with a nice salad and corn bread.

INGRID PITT'S
VAMPIRE BROTH

Pitt is best known as the seductive vampire Mircalla in *The Vampire Lovers*. She broke into the limelight with a role as an agent who assists Clint Eastwood and Richard Burton in *Where Eagles Dare*. Pitt went on to do some of the better 1970's British horror films, including *Countess Dracula*, *The House That Dripped Blood* and *The Wicker Man*. Pitt continues to act, write and has a cookbook of her own on the way.

The Transylvanian Diet.

The food I cook tends to be heavy on spices and rigid with garlic. Don't believe all that guff about vampires and garlic. That was put out by a particularly nasty little lycanthrophobe with piles that a gibbon would envy. And the grub has got to be plain and plentiful. One of the problems is finding the right ingredients. O.K. so virgin's blood is rare these days. Did it deter the residents of Summer Isle?

Not on your *Nosferatu*. They just enticed the last virgin of the western world and served him up flambéed to Christopher Lee. Me, I would have preferred a prime Angus steak but I was only there to display the body. With virgin's blood a no-no, what do we have that can at least bring a gleam to the eye and kick-start the pampered taste-buds?

How about Borscht?

How about the economy in Papua, New Guinea for that matter but let's not confuse the issue. Borscht (or Virgin

SELECTED GENRE FILMOGRAPHY

**INGRID PITT
(1937-)**

TV:

Doctor Who (1972)

Thriller (1973)

Flesh and Blood: The Hammer Heritage of Horror (1994)

Urban Gothic (2000)

Bride of Monster Mania (2000)

The Perfect Scary Movie (2005)

FEATURES:

The Sound of Horror (1964)

The Omegans (1968)

The House That Dripped Blood (1970)

The Vampire Lovers (1970)

Countess Dracula (1971)

The Wicker Man (1973)

Artemis 81 (1981)

Underworld (1985)

The Asylum (2000)

Minotaur (2005)

Sea of Dust (2006)

Vampire Broth if you want to be romantic) is one of the great soups of Eastern Europe.

RECIPE FOR A COVEN OF 4!

INGREDIENTS

6 uncooked beetroot (about 2 pounds) washed and peeled (they make a lovely, bloody mess on your hands and anything else in the kitchen they come in contact with)

4 medium sized onions, skinned and chopped (Vlad Tapes style)

1 tin concentrated onion soup. (and if you're not concentrating you're liable to cut your hand on the tin. Then you might regret who's coming to dinner)

9 cups seasoned beef stock

Butter

3 lemons

Salt and pepper

Sour cream (I always look at it before I put my face on in the morning — that would sour anything)

Chives (optional)

DIRECTIONS

The beetroot must be raw when it's committed to the pot. Cooking time can be reduced if beets are grated. Melt butter in saucepan and stir-fry chopped onions. Add beef stock and peeled beetroot and cook until tender (about 45 minutes). Remove from pot. Cut up and chop beetroot finely. Put in grater and mash if creamy texture is desired. Another opportunity to add real blood to the recipe. Those beet roots are slippery little sods.

Return mixture to stock, now red with beetroot juice and grated finger and add tin of onion soup. Beat all the time with whisk, a chance to wear that new Dominatrix rubber gear your Igor bought you for Christmas. Reheat broth gently, slowly (so get the rubber gear off.) Add lemon juice, salt and pepper to taste. Or if you want authenticity, invite a Russian around and strain the mixture through his socks. Serve chilled or hot with three or four tablespoons of sour cream and chopped chives. If this doesn't get you into The Federated Association of Dubious Dentures — nothing will.

ANGELA CARTWRIGHT'S
SECRET BEER AND CHEDDAR CHEESE SOUP

Angela Cartwright is best known for her television work including *Make Room For Daddy* and as Penny Robinson in the classic tv show *Lost in Space*. Cartwright had a breakthrough role, as Brigitta in the Robert Wise film, *The Sound of Music*.

Here's a soup that's "out of this world" and is one of my very favorites. It has become a tradition in my family every holiday season where I've been serving it to family and friends for over 20 years.

INGREDIENTS

¾	cup real butter	2	cups Cheddar cheese (sharp)
½	cup ⅛ inch diced celery	2	tablespoons Parmesan cheese
½	cup ⅛ inch diced carrots	¼	teaspoon Lawry's seasoning
½	cup ⅛ inch diced onion	1	can beer, flat
½	cup flour		Salt and pepper
4½	cups chicken stock or chicken broth		
½	teaspoon dry mustard		

DIRECTIONS

Sauté vegetables until done but not browned. Blend slowly flour, dry mustard, and chicken stock. Cook 5 minutes. Blend in Cheddar cheese, Parmesan cheese, and beer. Let simmer 20 minutes. Season and serve with French Bread and tossed salad.

Serves: 4 to 6

"I HOPE SHE DOES THE SOUP THING. IT'S ALWAYS A HOOT, AND WE DON'T ALL DIE FROM IT."
- WASH (ALAN TUDYK)
FIREFLY (2002)

SELECTED GENRE FILMOGRAPHY

ANGELA CARTWRIGHT (1952-)

www.angela-cartwright.com

TV:

Alfred Hitchcock Presents (1955)

Lost in Space (1965-1968)

Logan's Run (1977)

FEATURES:

The Fantasy Worlds of Irwin Allen (as Herself): (1995)

Lost in Space (1998)

Lost in Space Forever (archive footage): (1998)

SELECTED GENRE FILMOGRAPHY

ALFRED HITCHCOCK
(1899-1980)

TV:

Alfred Hitchcock Presents
(1955)

The Alfred Hitchcock Hour
(1962)

FEATURES:

Psycho (1960)

The Birds (1963)

ALFRED HITCHCOCK'S
VICHYSSOISE

Alfred Hitchcock is widely regarded as one, if not the, greatest and most influential film director of all time. He directed some of the most important cinematic thrillers, including *Psycho* and *The Birds*, not to mention his long running television shows, which he hosted: *Alfred Hitchcock Presents* and *The Alfred Hitchcock Hour*. His daughter Patricia acted in many of his films and TV shows.

INGREDIENTS

2	onions	6	cups chicken broth
3	leeks, white part only	3	cups heavy cream
6	potatoes, peeled and sliced		Pinch nutmeg
2	tablespoons flour		Salt
½	pound butter		White pepper
			Chives

DIRECTIONS

Cook the onions and leeks in butter over low heat in a large saucepan. Put these and the potatoes into the broth. Thicken with the flour. Cook for 40 minutes until the potatoes have fallen apart. Blend until smooth and allow to cool. Add cream, and salt to taste. Before serving, sprinkle with chopped chives and a little nutmeg.

> "IT WILL BE THE END OF ALL KITCHENS AND ALL COOKING. JUST A LITTLE STRIP OF WONKA'S MAGIC CHEWING GUM IS ALL YOU EVER NEED AT BREAKFAST, LUNCH AND DINNER. THIS PIECE OF GUM HAPPENS TO BE TOMATO SOUP, ROAST BEEF AND BLUEBERRY PIE."
>
> - WILLY WONKA (JOHNNY DEPP) ON HIS NEWEST PRODUCT.
> *CHARLIE AND THE CHOCOLATE FACTORY (2005)*

VERONICA CARTWRIGHT'S
MUSHROOM CREAM SOUP

Born in Bristol, England, Veronica is the older sister of Angela Cartwright. Veronica began work in television in the late 1950's and played Cathy Brenner in Alfred Hitchcock's *The Birds*. Cartwright also appeared in original *Twilight Zone* and *One Step Beyond* television episodes. She went on to star in landmark 70's classics *Alien* and *Invasion of the Body Snatchers*.

INGREDIENTS

2	tablespoons butter
2	tablespoons minced onion
1½	pounds white mushrooms, cleaned and sliced
1	teaspoon lemon juice
3	cups chicken broth

Mushrooms, sliced for garnish

1	tablespoon minced parsley
½	cup heavy (35%) cream
2	egg yolks

Salt and pepper

DIRECTIONS

Melt butter in a large non aluminum pan. Add onions, sliced mushrooms and lemon juice. Sauté over low heat until mushrooms are tender (not browned) and onion is limp. Add broth, parsley and simmer for 25-30 minutes. Pureé soup in a blender and return to pan. In a small bowl whisk the cream with the egg yolks until well blended. Stir the cream mixture into the soup and cook stirring constantly for 2 minutes or until thickened. Season to taste with salt and pepper.

Serves: 4 to 6

"THERE'S AN EYE IN ME SOUP."
- FINNIS EVERGLOT (ALBERT FINNEY)
CORPSE BRIDE (2005)

KERWIN MATHEWS'S
HENRI SOUL 'S "POULE AU POT"

Born in Janesville, Wisconsin, Mathews was originally a teacher before taking on the duties of Captain Sinbad in *The 7th Voyage of Sinbad*. Mathews, always a leading man, went on to star in *The 3 Worlds of Gulliver*, *Jack the Giant Killer*, *Maniac* and *Nightmare in Blood*. Mathews now retired, resides in San Francisco with his beloved cats.

INGREDIENTS

1   3-pound chicken

3   carrots scraped, quartered lengthwise and cut into 1½ inch lengths

3   ribs celery trimmed, split lengthwise and cut into 1½ inch lengths

2   or 3 turnips about half a pound trimmed and cut into pieces of the same shape as the celery and carrots

Salt and freshly ground pepper

1   cup leaks, white sections only, quartered lengthwise and cut into 1½ inch lengths

1   fennel bulb cut into ¼ inch slices

1   zucchini, trimmed, quartered and cut into 1½ inch links

5   cups fresh or canned chicken broth

¼   cup rice

Chervil for garnish

DIRECTIONS

Truss the chicken and place it in a kettle. It should fit in the pot snugly or else too much water must be added and the soup will be weak and watery. Cover with water, and add carrots, celery, turnips, leeks, fennel and zucchini. Bring to a boil, remove from heat and drain well.

Return chicken in kettle and add chicken broth. Add all vegetables, except zucchini. Simmer 20 minutes uncovered. Add zucchini, and simmer 5 minutes longer, skimming foam from top periodically.

Add rice, salt and pepper. Cook until chicken is tender, about 10 minutes.

Un-truss the chicken. Cut it into serving pieces, serve in 4 hot soup bowls with equal amounts of vegetables and rice in each bowl. Garnish with fresh chervil.

Serves: 4 to 6

ALLAN CAILLOU'S
TARRAGON SALAD DRESSING

INGREDIENTS

½	cup red wine	1	teaspoon salt
½	cup vinegar	2	garlic cloves minced
2	tablespoons of lemon juice	2	cups olive oil
1	teaspoon sugar		Hefty splash of
½	cup tarragon leaves		Worcestershire sauce

DIRECTIONS

Chop fresh tarragon leaves finely or use one tablespoon of dried tarragon powder.

Whisk ingredients thoroughly, while slowly adding the oil. Put into a corked bottle and shake the hell out of it. It's ready now; best to keep it in the fridge.

"NO, SILLY. CONSUMMATE IS A KIND OF SOUP."
- BRANDI ALEXANDER (CINDY ROUBAL)
BLOOD FEAST 2: ALL U CAN EAT (2002)

MEAL SCENES

Freaks (1932)

A wedding feast for freak carnival performers.

Dawn of the Dead (1979)

A lovely dinner sequence smack dab in the middle of a blood and guts horror movie.

The Exorcist (1974)

Pea soup was used in the famous spewing scene because Linda Blair hated the vegetable soup they had used originally.

Edward Scissorhands (1990)

Edward (Johnny Depp) gets to sample Joyce's (Kathy Baker) ambrosia salad and everything else at a summer BBQ.

SELECTED GENRE FILMOGRAPHY

CAREL STRUYCKEN
(1948 -)

TV:

Star Trek: The Next Generation (1987)

Twin Peaks (1990)

Babylon 5 (1994)

Star Trek: Voyager (1995)

FEATURES:

Ewoks: The Battle for Endor (1985)

The Witches of Eastwick (1987)

The Addams Family (1991)

Science Fiction (2002)

Addams Family Values (1993)

Journey to the Center of the Earth (1993)

"AH, THE LEAKY CAULDRON! IF YOU HAVE THE PEA SOUP, MAKE SURE YOU EAT IT BEFORE IT EATS YOU!"

- SHRUNKEN HEAD

HARRY POTTER AND THE PRISONER OF AZKABAN (2004)

POSSESSED PEA SOUP

INGREDIENTS

2	cups split green peas	1	teaspoon dried thyme
10	cups water	1	ham bone
4	onions diced	1	bay leaf
1	teaspoon garlic powder	¼	cup Havarti, grated
	Parsley		Salt and pepper

DIRECTIONS

Rinse peas before using but do not soak them. Remove all of the fat from the ham bone. Combine ingredients in a large pot and bring to a boil. Simmer for 1½ to 2 hours. During this time the soup may talk back to you. It's best to just ignore it. Remove the bay leaf before serving. Garnish with fresh parsley and sprinkle top with the Havarti cheese. For a smooth soup, puree it in a blender. This soup freezes well and is best made a day ahead.

CAREL STRUYCKEN'S SALAD DRESSING

Though he studied to be a film-maker at the American Film Institute, Struycken turned to acting instead. He was born in The Netherlands and is most recognizable as Lurch in the *Addams Family* films. Struycken, who is approximately 7 feet tall, is a strict vegetarian. Star Trek fans best know Struycken as Majel Barret's valet, Mr. Homn in episodes of *Star Trek: The Next Generation*.

To make 1 cup of salad dressing:

Virgin olive oil and balsamic vinegar (ratio 45% olive oil, 55% balsamic), about two or three shakes of Worcestershire sauce, Italian herbs, a heaping teaspoon of Poupon or similar mustard and some salt. Shake well.

MICHAEL BERRYMAN'S
SALAD

Berryman is best known as Pluto in the classic Wes Craven chiller *The Hills Have Eyes*. Berryman, has used his features to his advantage in other horror films including *Deadly Blessing, Evil Spirits* and several television shows such as *Tales From the Crypt*. Berryman, a gourmet cook in his own right, continues to act and lives in Los Angeles.

"It's a light meal with a lot of protein and it gets you through the day! "

INGREDIENTS

Butter lettuce

Heirloom tomatoes

Kalamata olives

Feta cheese

Hard boiled egg

Tuna

Avocado

Whole clove of garlic (roasted)

Red bell pepper, julienned

Bermuda onion—sliced thin and deep fried.

Tofu (optional)

DIRECTIONS

Place butter lettuce in a bowl and add tomatoes and olives. Sprinkle feta cheese on top and add tuna. Add avocado and sprinkle feta on top. Add the garlic and red pepper and egg. Add a layer of Bermuda onion and tofu.

Pour a homemade dressing: extra virgin olive oil, and vinegar or use store bought. A light dressing is best, because you don't want something that will smother all the various flavors.

Serve with whole wheat bread sticks or sourdough bread.

Bon appetit!

BEN CHAPMAN'S
THE GILLMAN'S LAGOON SALAD SUPREME

Chapman a Korean War veteran cemented his place in movie lore as one of two actors to play the creature in the original *Creature from the Black Lagoon*. Chapman's scenes were filmed in Hollywood. Chapman keeps busy with occasional convention appearances and resides in Hawaii.

INGREDIENTS

1   package small elbow macaroni

1   package slivered almonds

1   cup diced celery

1   package imitation lobster chunks

¼   cup diced onions

1   package imitation crab (can be substituted for real lobster and crab)

DRESSING:

1   cup mayonnaise

1   teaspoon curry powder

DIRECTIONS

Cook the elbow macaroni in boiling water no more than 10 minutes. Do not overcook. (el dente style — chewy)

Drain well after rinsing in cold water.

Mix all ingredients in large salad bowl.

Fold in mixture of mayonnaise and curry powder.

The amount of dressing is personal preference and taste.

"ALL YOU BOYS SEEMED TO HAVE LEARNED IS THAT CAESAR IS A 'SALAD DRESSING DUDE.'"

- MR. RYAN (BERNIE CASEY) ON BILL AND TED'S LACK OF HISTORICAL KNOW-HOW.

BILL & TED'S EXCELLENT ADVENTURE (1989)

DICK DUROCK'S
ROASTED BELL PEPPER AND BLACK BEAN SALAD

Durock, who is 6' 6", served with the US Marines, before working in Hollywood as a stunt man and actor. He played a pie eating champ in *Stand by Me* and has had bits in the original *Star Trek* and *Battlestar Galactica* television series. Durock is often associated with his work as the title character in *Swamp Thing* in the original films and television series.

INGREDIENTS

2	medium size red bell peppers (you can use bottled peppers if you wish... Make sure they're roasted)
½	cup rice wine vinegar (unseasoned)
¼	cup extra virgin olive oil
1	tablespoon honey

½	teaspoon chili oil (optional)
¼	cup minced cilantro
⅛	cup green onions, chopped
3	cans black beans, rinsed and drained (very important)

Cilantro sprigs

Salt and pepper

DIRECTIONS

Roast peppers on grill or gas stove top until blackened. Cool and remove blackened skin. Cut into strips or chunks. Of course if you use bottled peppers just drain well and cut.

In a glass bowl mix together oil, vinegar, honey, minced cilantro and green onions. If using chili oil add now. Mix in drained beans and roasted peppers. Season with salt and pepper to taste.

Garnish with cilantro sprigs.

This one's a keeper... Enjoy.

SELECTED GENRE FILMOGRAPHY

DICK DUROCK

www.dickdurock.com

TV:

Stunts:
Quark (1977)

Buck Rogers in the 25th Century (1979)

Actor:
Star Trek (1966)

Battlestar Galactica (1978)

The Incredible Hulk (1978)

Knight Rider (1982)

Swamp Thing (1990)

FEATURES:

Stunts:
Conquest of the Planet of the Apes (1972)

Battle For the Planet of the Apes (1973)

Doc Savage: The Man of Bronze (1975)

The Sword and the Sorcerer (1982)

The Monster Squad (1987)

Actor:
The Dark Secrets of Harvest Home (1978)

More Wild Wild West (1980)

Swamp Thing (1982)

The Return of Swamp Thing (1989)

Delirious (1991)

JAMES HONG'S
ULTIMATE SALAD

James Hong studied civil engineering before switching gears and turning to acting. Hong's career lists a staggering 450 plus films. Hong is well known to genre fans as Dr. Chew in *Bladerunner* and the evil sorcerer Lo Pan in John Carpenter's *Big Trouble in Little China*.

INGREDIENTS

2 spoonfuls of eyeballs

5 fingers of fingers

2 tomatoes, blonds preferably

DIRECTIONS

Mix thoroughly in blood vinegar dressing and you too shall be Ultimate! Forever!

Best food ever: *Hawaii 5-0*: Four long tables of Hawaiian and American food.

Worst food ever: A couple of low budget films long ago where they had McDonald's, Kentucky Fried Chicken and Dominoes Pizza for supper.

DIANA MILLAY'S
ANGEL HAIR, CRAB AND MUSHROOM SALAD

Best known for her portrayal of Laura Collins in the long running vampire television saga, *Dark Shadows*, Millay also writes and has just self-published a cookbook. She has also worked in many genre related television shows including *Thriller* and *The Man from U.N.C.L.E.*

INGREDIENTS

8	ounces angel hair pasta	2	tablespoons wine vinegar
1	tablespoon butter	2	tablespoons soy sauce
1	portabella mushroom, cut up	5	young scallions, finely chopped (reserve green tops)
¼	cup tartar sauce	1	pound lump crabmeat, flaked
1	tablespoon sesame oil		

DIRECTIONS

Prepare pasta according to directions on package and cool.

Sauté mushroom in butter and set aside.

Slice green scallion tops lengthwise into very thin strips and add to mushrooms.

Finely chop white part of scallions.

Whisk together: tartar sauce, sesame oil, vinegar, soy sauce and finely chopped white part of scallions. Add crabmeat to sauce and combine with cool pasta. Chill briefly before serving.

Serves: 4

SELECTED GENRE FILMOGRAPHY

DIANA MILLAY (1935-   )

TV:

Thriller (1961)

The Man From U.N.C.L.E. (1964)

Dark Shadows (1966-1967 1969)

FEATURES:

Tarzan and the Great River (1967)

Night of Dark Shadows (1971)

Dark Shadows 30th Anniversary Tribute (1996) (as Herself).

BEST SOUP SCENES

Soup scenes we love!

Batman (1989) — Michael Keaton and Kim Basinger eat soup across an abnormally spacious table setting.

ExistenZ (1999) — Ted Pikul (Jude Law) assembles a gun out of gristle from the contents of his soup then uses it to kill the waiter in this surreal tale by director David Cronenberg.

Indiana Jones and The Temple of Doom (1984) — Willie (Kate Capshaw) is not fond of the food at the Danquot Palace. She glances into her soup… that glances back.

Lemony Snicket: A Series of Unfortunate Events (2004) — Living on the edge of a cliff can make one rather edgy. (Meryl Streep) warns the children to eat only cold cucumber soup as hot soup is far too dangerous.

Mysterious Island (1961) — After washing up on a beach, a balloon crash survivor (Gary Merrill) plans to make an oyster stew. When serving it to two drop dead beautiful women he offers them the "seafood soup, like a French bouillabaisse."

The Nightmare Before Christmas (1993) — A wheelchair bound Dr. Finklestein demands soup from Sally, the poor ragdoll. She poisons his soup with Deadly Nightshade and adds Frog's Breath to cover the odor.

The Sixth Sense (1999) — A video tape reveals just what's been happening to Kyra Collins's soup.

Being John Malkovich (1999) — In what must be the weirdest restaurant scene in history, John Malkovich enters his own head and finds himself in a restaurant where all the patrons and waiters look like him and he's the only thing on the menu.

Young Frankenstein (1974) — A blind man (Gene Hackman) is ecstatic to welcome a visitor to his home unaware that it just happens to be one Frankenstein monster (Peter Boyle). All goes well until the blind man pours the hot soup in the wrong place in one of the films funniest scenes.

The Others (2000) — Two young children discuss ghosts during a candlelit pea soup dinner.

MEATLESS

"ANY THOUGHTS AS TO WHY ANYBODY WOULD BE GROWING CORN IN THE MIDDLE OF THE DESERT?"

- DANA SCULLY (GILLIAN ANDERSON) TO FOX MULDER.

THE X FILES (1998)

KRISTEN CLOKE'S
CORNCAKES

Born in Van Nuys California, Cloke attended California State University where she studied psychology. She took theatre courses and she decided to pursue acting full time. Known to fans as Shane Vansen on *Space: Above and Beyond*. She writes, directs and produces plays for of a repertory theatre company in Burbank, California. She is married to *Space: Above and Beyond* producer Glen Morgan.

These corncakes are low in fat which is important to those of us who care.

INGREDIENTS

3	egg whites, slightly beaten	⅓	cup scallions (including ⅓ green) chopped
¼	cup flour	⅓	cup red bell peppers, diced
¼	teaspoon salt		
	Pepper	5	tablespoons fat free sour cream (or regular if you prefer)
2	cups uncooked corn cut from the cob, or 10 ounce frozen corn, thawed	5	tablespoons salsa

DIRECTIONS

In a large bowl, combine egg whites, flour, salt and pepper. Add the corn, scallions and red pepper and stir. Heat a non stick skillet over medium heat and spray lightly with cooking spray. Spoon about two tablespoons of the corn mixture into the pan to make a 3 inch corn cake. Cook 2 to 3 minutes on each side until lightly golden. Serve with sour cream and salsa.

MEAL MOVIE SPOTLIGHT!

Village of the Giants (1965)

A young genius accidentally invents a substance (*see Goo Cake page 190*) that causes all life to grow. Seeing the potential for money, his sister and her boyfriend have other plans, eat it and grow to enormous size and take over a town.

ALFRED HITCHCOCK'S
POTATO SOUFFL

This is very old fashioned and simple. Double fried potatoes.

Peel 6-8 Spanish Floury potatoes and wipe them dry. Then cut them into round slices 3 millimeters thick. Place each slice on a paper towel to dry.

Heat fat in two deep-frying saucepans. One must be hot but not boiling, and the potato-slices should be plunged into it and remain 7 or 8 minutes. Be careful!

Then drain the fat quickly from the potato-slices and plunge them into the second saucepan which must be boiling.

The potato slices swell; and when they are golden-brown and firm, let them drain and sprinkle them with salt.

FOOD QUOTES OF ALFRED HITCHCOCK

"For me, the cinema is not a slice of life, but a piece of cake."

"I beg permission to mention by name only four people who have given me the most affection, appreciation, and encouragement, and constant collaboration. The first of the four is a film editor, the second is a scriptwriter, the third is the mother of my daughter Pat, and the fourth is as fine a cook as ever performed miracles in a domestic kitchen. And their names are Alma Reville." — accepting his American Film Institute Life Achievement award.

"A murder without gleaming scissors is like asparagus without the hollandaise sauce — tasteless."

"A good film is when the price of the dinner, the theatre admission and the babysitter were worth it."

"Conversation is the enemy of good wine and food."

"Some of our most exquisite murders have been domestic, performed with tenderness in simple, homey places like the kitchen table."

"I once gave a dinner party many years ago where all the food was blue. It was a full meal. It was chicken soup-blue; blue trout; blue chicken; blue ice cream and when you broke open your roll the bread was blue inside" — on the Dick Cavett Show (1972).

"HAVE A POTATO. HAVE A POTATO."
- HORACE FEMM (ERNEST THESIGER)
OLD DARK HOUSE (1932)

**"THE ONLY THING
I LIKE BETTER
THAN AN EGGPLANT
BURGER IS A
CHOCOLATE COVERED
EGGPLANT BURGER."**

- SHAGGY (MATTHEW
LILLARD)
SCOOBY DOO (2000)

KIM HUNTER'S
EGGPLANT CASSEROLE

Kim Hunter starred as Stella Kowalski on Broadway in *A Streetcar Named Desire* and won an Oscar for the role in the film version. Her first major role was as David Niven's wife in the Michael Powell fantasy *A Matter of Life and Death*. She left an indelible impression with her role as an inquisitive scientist in *Planet of the Apes*.

INGREDIENTS

1	teaspoon sweet basil	2	(8-ounce) cans tomato sauce
¼	teaspoon oregano	2	(4 1/2 ounce) cans chopped black olives
4	Medium-sized eggplants	1	pound medium Tillamook cheese, grated (or use mild Cheddar cheese, if Tillamook is unavailable)
1½	to 2 tablespoons oil		
2	large cloves garlic, finely chopped		
1	large white onion, diced		salt and freshly ground black pepper to taste
½	large green pepper, diced		flour
4	eggs separated		

DIRECTIONS

Crush the basil and oregano in mortar until powdery. Slice the eggplants, peel them, and then cut into cubes. Put the cubes in a large pot, cover with boiling water, and cook until transparent. When the eggplant is done, drain thoroughly, and mash the cubes in a mixing bowl. (If a potato masher doesn't get all the lumps out, use an electric hand beater briefly.)

In the meantime, heat 1½ to 2 tablespoons oil in a heavy skillet, and add half the chopped garlic, onion, and green pepper. Sauté until soft, about 20 minutes. Add the tomato sauce, two cans of water, the basil, oregano, and salt and pepper to taste. Put the skillet on a back burner and let it simmer very slowly until ready to use.

Add the remaining chopped garlic, onion, and green pepper to the mashed eggplant, and blend. Add enough flour to thicken the mixture so it will hold a firm ball on a spoon.

Beat the egg yolks and blend into the eggplant mixture. Add salt and pepper to taste. Beat the whites until they form peaks, and then fold into the mixture.

Heat oil or fat in a large, heavy skillet, enough to come up the sides about half an inch. Drop heaping tablespoons full of the eggplant mixture into the hot fat, four or five at a time, and mash them down with a spatula to make a patty. Fry them to a golden brown on both sides.

Using a slotted spatula, drain the patties well, and place them close together in layers on an ovenproof platter or on a 13x9 by 2-inch baking dish. Top each layer with the tomato sauce, chopped olives, and grated cheese.
(2 to 4 layers, depending on the size of your eggplants.)

Bake at 350°F for 30 minutes.

Serves: 8

The whole dish can be prepared a day ahead, ready to bake. Just refrigerate it. Actually, it's better to do it ahead. The flavors have more time to blend. Either remove from the fridge to reach room temperature before baking, or put it straight into the oven and add to the baking time. The casserole should be piping hot before serving.

VEGETABLE TRIVIA

Close Encounter of the Third Kind (1977)

During the dinner scene where Roy (Richard Dreyfuss) piles up the mashed potatoes, the young actress who plays his daughter says there is a fly in her potato. This was not in the script and the cast and crew had to keep from laughing.

Empire Strikes Back (1980)

The chase through the asteroid field is one of the most breathtaking scenes. One of the asteroids that flies past the Millenium Falcon is actually a potato. Shot by effects cameraman Ken Ralston, some of the asteroids include chewing gum and an old tennis show.

Charlie and the Chocolate Factory (2005)

One of the buttons on the glass elevator reads "Spewed Vegetables."

Lord of the Rings: The Fellowship of the Rings (2001)

In order to create a convincing Hobbit village, 5000 cubic meters of vegetables and plants were grown a year before filming commenced.

VINCENT PRICE
RISOTTO CON PISELLI E LA LATTUGA

Born in St. Louis, Missouri, Price, a gourmet cook, writer and well respected actor became a fixture of atmospheric horror movies since co-starring with Boris Karloff in *The Tower of London*. Price worked in a slew of films for Roger Corman many of them Edgar Allen Poe adaptations. Price portrayed Egghead in the *Batman* television series and wrote a number of cookbooks with his wife Mary Grant.

This is a foolproof recipe for Risotto courtesy of Price's daughter Victoria.

INGREDIENTS

6	cups chicken or vegetable broth
6	cloves garlic
½	white or yellow onion
½	cup arborio rice
1	stick (½ cup) butter
	Olive oil as needed

Dry vermouth

⅓ cup grated Parmesan cheese

1 head Boston, bibb or romaine lettuce (3 cups shredded)

1 cup shelled fresh peas or defrosted frozen peas

DIRECTIONS

CONDIMENTI: Heat two tablespoons butter with a dash of olive oil in small skillet over moderate heat. When it begins to foam, add the peas and cook for 3 to 5 minutes, stirring occasionally. Turn off heat and set aside.

BRODO: Bring broth to a steady simmer in a saucepan on top of the stove. Leave on back burner at low flame.

SOFFRITO: Finely chop onions and garlic and place in large, heavy saucepan. Coat thoroughly with olive oil and sauté at moderate heat for 3 minutes or until onions become translucent. Be careful not to brown them.

RISO: Add the rice to the soffrito; using a wooden spoon, stir for 1 minute, making sure all the grains are well coated. Together, add small portions of the brodo, ¼ to ½ cup, and handfuls of lettuce. When adding the brodo, be sure to keep stirring so all the liquid is completely absorbed and the lettuce begins to dissolve. When each portion is thoroughly assimilated into the mixture, add more. Keep on with this technique until rice is tender but

firm. At this point, come the final touches: Step by step add all of the peas, butter, vermouth, and Parmesan. The texture should be creamy. These final steps give your dish the desired taste and texture.

VICTORIA PRICE
...ON VINCENT PRICE

My Dad always loved to eat. That was the main thing. He loved all different kinds of food and his mother was a wonderful cook. But I would have to say that his taste in food was not as adventurous as it became at the end of his life. It wasn't until he and my mother started traveling. They saw themselves as collectors, so they extended the idea of collection to recipes. They'd go to restaurants and they would ask to meet the chef or if they liked a particular dish asked for the recipe. That's how it started. So they wrote the cookbook, *The Treasury of Great Recipes* in 1965 and all of a sudden everyone was interested in my father as a cook. They didn't want my mother who might have actually been the better cook to appear on the talk shows, so they asked my father and all of a sudden he had to learn more and more about cooking, but it came as a natural interest to him.

He learned more and more and became one of the founding members of the American Food and Wine Institute. He wrote two other cookbooks with my mother. He appeared on a number of talk shows and really became known as the cook he is known to be today.

He was a passionate cook. He cooked certain things incredibly well and other things he wanted to learn to cook that well, so he would practice and practice. I remember as a kid it seemed to me we had ratatouille for a year straight!

In January of 1983 I spent a month with him and he decided he wanted to learn how to perfect Crème Brule. That meant that we would make a big Pyrex pan of Crème Brule every other day. Then we'd have to eat it. I went off to college 20 pounds fatter. He would get on these cooking jags.

He was a little frustrated with me. I didn't have the aptitude for cooking. He had this funny habit. I'd say, "God Dad. This is a great meal. How do you make that?" He'd say, "You take two pounds of flour and add this and do that and add this ingredient and that ingredient. It's really very simple." That tells me nothing. He really only taught me how to make three things, popovers, which are very simple; pancakes which are also very simple, but require an art to get perfect and rissole.

He loved bread and baking any kind of bread. I definitely inherited that love of bread. One of his most memorable encounters; he was at a small dinner party and in walked Greta Garbo. He was just blown away. He didn't know what to talk to her about and he ended up next to her at the cocktails party before the dinner and he started talking to her about breaking bread, because he had read somewhere that she was a health nut. That went on for 15 minutes. They had this great conversation. Then they parted and all of a sudden he realized he was sitting next to her at dinner, so they started in on bread again and talked about bread for the entire dinner.

A few years later, he was walking down the street in New York and was tapped on the shoulder and he thought "oh it's probably a fan" and he turned around and it was Greta Garbo. She said, "Wasn't that a wonderful evening we had that night?"

He had favorite restaurants in various cities. In San Francisco he loved a local restaurant called Momma's which was an Italian restaurant on Knob Hill, so it wasn't always exalted tastes, although Momma's is a really good Italian restaurant it wasn't like he had to pick the trendiest restaurant.

He did all the shopping. The funny thing about my Dad was that he could be very thrifty with how he spent his money on certain things. But if he walked into a grocery store and there were chanterelle mushrooms at twenty dollars a pound he wouldn't hesitate to buy them, but he wouldn't buy a good pair of socks. He never had a good car until the end of his life.

He made a great cassoulet, and soufflés were difficult to make, and he made very good soufflés. His were perfect, that great light consistency with that pungent flavor. He nailed the soufflés.

He loved a good beer. He loved California wine, but often at the end of his life, when we'd go to an Italian restaurant you'd think he would order a fine glass of wine, although he would love a great Chianti or something like that, but he loved amoretti beer, dose chi's and Negor model, the dark Mexican beer. He liked to drink in general, but he loved to drink beer.

"AN INTELLECTUAL CARROT. THE MIND BOGGLES."
- NED "SCOTTY" SCOTT

THE THING FROM ANOTHER WORLD (1951)

He liked liver, onions, anything with garlic, salad, bread, so you can tell he was a man of healthy appetites.

Tower of London was only his second movie, so there he was with Boris Karloff and Basil Rathbone and in one scene, they were supposed to get drunk, but they were drinking Coke. And they drank a lot of Coca-Cola throughout this scene. Finally they were supposed to throw my father in this vat of malmsey wine. Boris and Basil as a joke, did this because he was a rookie actor. They threw everything, old cigarette butts etc... It must have been disgusting down in this vat of water. They threw him down there and he had to go under and hang onto a bar at the bottom for a full ten second count with all this crap floating around. Finally they pulled him out and my Dad looked around for Boris and Basil and he was wondering, "Why aren't they here? I'm finished. This is my last scene in the movie." Then they came out and congratulated him on doing so well and presented him with a case of Coca-Cola.

My Dad never spent any money to go on a vacation for himself. If he wanted to go to Italy he found a way to make three bad movies there, so he could be in Italy for six months.

Somebody, probably my step-mother, talked him into taking Marcella Hisan's class on Italian cooking at the Chiprioni in Venice. It was the best thing he ever did. Victor Hisan, her husband, is an Italian wine expert, so it was a combo Italian cooking, Italian wine course. He became good friends with Victor and Marcella. The best thing, favorite thing he learned in that class was how to make risotto. Risotto is one of these tricky dishes, because it seems like it's easy, but it requires sort of the right touch to get the ingredients just perfect, so you don't have glop in the pan. It requires patience. You have to be willing to stand there and stir. He loved doing it. He wrote everything down. He bought risotto cookbooks. At the end of his life he lost his taste buds, which was really, really difficult for somebody who loved to eat and he became very thin. He probably weighed what I do and he was 6'4." He looked really boney.

He found the only thing he could enjoy was risotto. I think there was something about the density of it that felt satisfying, kind of a stick to your ribs thing, but also that the flavor in risotto; there were some strong flavors that he couldn't enjoy, but there was a subtlety to risotto that he still could enjoy. But he didn't really have the patience every night to cook it so he taught me how to cook it was kind of an exacting and laborious process, because he wasn't satisfied if I got "close." If someone else was going to cook risotto it had to be right. Finally I figured out how to do it and there was an additional problem that I don't eat dairy products. I can eat parmesan, but I can't have heavy cream, so I could do the butter and the parmesan (we made that compromise), but I couldn't do the heavy cream, so he had to figure out how to get that same taste that he loved without the heavy cream. We figured it out by experimenting. He loved to make a celery risotto, which you wouldn't think would be good for someone with impaired taste buds, but he thought it was so subtle and it turned this very pale shade of green and then every so often on a special occasion we would add peas to it, so it would, so it would be a celery and pea risotto. So that's the one I'm going to give you.

POTATOES DIJON

This recipe makes a great side dish with any meat dish or could be made into a salad. This is best made a day ahead.

INGREDIENTS

2	pounds baby purple potatoes, halved	2	yellow peppers finely diced
3	red onions, diced	½	pound turkey bacon, chopped
2	red peppers		
4	tablespoons of mayonnaise (real not whipped)	3	tablespoons of Dijon mustard
		4	tablespoons fresh basil, chopped

DIRECTIONS

Add potatoes to a pot of salted water and cook for 10-15 minutes.

Fry the bacon in a pan. Allow to cool somewhat, drain the bacon drippings and set aside. Crumble the bacon and place in a small bowl, with the onion, peppers, mayonnaise and mustard.

Add hot potatoes to cold mix and stir with turkey bacon drippings.

Add basil immediately before serving.

RAE DAWN CHONG'S
CHEESE AND NUT LOAF

Born in Edmonton, Alberta, Chong is the daughter of comedian Tommy Chong. She first made an impact in *Quest for Fire* and has appeared in *Commando* with Arnold Schwarzenegger and Steven Spielberg's *The Color Purple*.

INGREDIENTS

½	cup walnuts	½	cup Gruyere
½	cup pecans	½	cup Stilton
½	cup pine nuts	½	cup cottage cheese
1	cup oatmeal	1	cup cornflakes
½	cup Asiago	4	eggs
		1	cup chopped mushrooms

GRAVY:

½	cup flour	½	cup brandy
3	tablespoons vegetable bouillon	1	onion
		1	garlic clove
2	cups water		

DIRECTIONS

Mix all ingredients in a bowl.

Pour sludge like mixture into a loaf pan.

Bake loaf for 1 hour or until done. Treat it like a cake.

TO MAKE THE GRAVY:

Brown the flour in a separate pan until dark, but not burnt.

Combine the flour with the bouillon and mix in 2 cups of boiling water and stir in sauce pan until dissolved.

Remove from heat and set aside.

In a clean pan, sauté onions and garlic until soft. Add bouillon water and brandy, reduce to half and add flour mixture slowly. Serve with gravy.

SELECTED GENRE FILMOGRAPHY

RAE DAWN CHONG (1961-)

TV:

Tall Tales and Legends (1985)

The Hitchhiker (1983)

The Outer Limits (1995)

Highlander (1992)

Poltergeist: The Legacy (1996)

Mysterious Ways (2000)

FEATURES:

Tales From the Darkside: The Movie (1990)

The Borrower (1991)

Time Runner (1993)

Starlight (1996)

Deadly Skies (2005)

ALFRED HITCHCOCK'S
YORKSHIRE PUDDING

This is Alfred Hitchcock's own no fail Yorkshire Pudding recipe. Serve with Roast Beef or serve with Booth Colman's Hussar Pot Roast. (page 153)

INGREDIENTS

2	eggs	½	teaspoon salt
1	cup milk	1	tablespoon shortening
1	cup flour		

DIRECTIONS

Put two eggs in a blender alone. Keep it going while you add the milk and salt. Keep it going while you add flour, teaspoon by teaspoon. Give it a final good whirl at top speed. Put blender and contents in refrigerator until ready to cook.

Put large tablespoon of shortening in a small baking pan and place in a 400°F oven. When the pan is very hot, take the blender from refrigerator, give it another good whirl at high speed for a moment then pour it into the hot pan with the shortening.

It should take about 15 minutes to rise. Leave in oven until it dries out. Once it has risen, you might be able to turn oven down to 350°F, but care should be taken about this.

"IT WORKED JACK. YOU JUST DIGESTED THE BAD GUY."

- TEMPLETON PUCK (DENNIS QUAID) TO MARTIN SHORT

INNERSPACE (1987)

SUSAN GORDON'S
SWEET RICE AND VEGETABLES

Daughter of Bert I. Gordon, born in St. Paul, Minnesota, had a small part in *Attack of the Puppet people* and went on to do many television shows and movies. Gordon is fondly remembered by fans as Jenny in *The Twilight Zone* episode, "The Fugitive" and films like *Tormented* and *The Boy and the Pirates*.

INGREDIENTS

1 cup sweet brown rice	1 cup sweet corn, fresh or frozen
1 cup brown rice	1 cup butternut squash, diced (about 1 cup)
1 large onion, diced (about 1 cup)	1 pinch sea salt
2 large carrots, diced (about 1 cup)	Toasted seeds
2 large celery stalks, diced (about 1 cup)	4 cups water

DIRECTIONS

Wash both kinds of rice together and soak overnight in four cups of (spring) water.

Place washed and soaked rice, together with the soaking water, in the bottom of a heavy-weight casserole dish.

Layer the diced vegetables on top of the rice in the order they are listed in the list above.

Over a medium-high flame, bring to a boil. Add a pinch of sea salt, cover the pot, reduce the heat to low, and simmer for 40 minutes. For best results, use a flame deflector under the pot.

When rice is done, consistency will be wet and slightly glutinous. Scoop into wooden bowl and cover with a bamboo mat, which will allow the rice to 'breathe.'

Sprinkle rice with gomashio (toasted sesame seeds grounded with sea salt) or other toasted pumpkin or sunflower seeds and steamed greens such as broccoli, broccoli rabe, kale, bok choy, or collards.

TALMAGE POWELL
...ON BEANS

The late Talmage Powell was a noted mystery novelist, who scripted a number of the *Alfred Hitchcock Presents* television episodes. Powell's last television script was for Roald Dahl's *Tales of the Unexpected*, entitled "Proxy" (1984).

What can I say about myself as a gourmet? Truth is, nothing, for the simple reason that I don't rate the nomer. However, no matter how bleak the skies, stygian the dark moment, I always have something to be thankful for.

I'm one of the creatures at the top of the food chain. Being thusly situated, I have tried a large variety derived from lower rungs of the food ladder, in New York, New Orleans, Hollywood, where supposedly magic lurks for the palate, to eateries in Houma, Louisiana, where I drank the best cuppa coffee in my life, the Star Cafe in Globe, Arizona, which set before me a steak to rival one I consumed in the diner of the Santa Fe railroad's Super Chief, and Jack's Cafe in Soperton, Georgia, where the barbecued ribs on the table should have made the place famous.

If it's part of the normal larder I'm almost sure to like it, whether it previously swam, grazed, or sprouted. I don't mind if the concept for its preparation came from Finland, Greece, Germany, Spain, England, Japan, China, et al. I like it best when it is prepared with a skill that brings out the natural goodness, and if that has occurred, keep your sauces, elixirs, and marinades. The lowly cabbage and carrot, for example, are a royal feast when a genius in the kitchen, such as my wife, exercises the secret of tapping the natural sugars to peak and at that singular instant placing the dish on the table.

Cooking is an art, and few there be who master it. The untalented may graduate cooking school, titled Chef, and remain lousy cooks. The artiste in the kitchen has never been in great supply, and the numbers are certainly dwindling in the generation that was weaned beneath the Golden Arches. Where do you go nowadays to eat a shrimp for its own natural succulence, a navy bean that requires no catsup?

Speaking of dried beans, even the chick pea is food royal, if prepared as in the days of the Columbia Restaurant in Ybor City, the Latin Quarter of Tampa Florida in the pre-boom-time era.

The Recipe

As a matter of fact, the entire family of dried beans, from chick pea to the princely large lima, rates highly among peasants such as myself. To cook a good bean, baby limas perhaps, wash a pound of the beans. While you're doing this, in a pot sufficiently large to hold the beans and water covering them two inches above their level, fry two thick slices of Virginia-cured bacon. Cook the bacon well done, then throw it away. Into the bacon pot-likker dump the beans and water, bring to a hard, rolling boil, turn off the heat, cover the pot, and let it stand 3 hours.

Finish cooking by adding a heaping teaspoon of salt and returning the bean pot to an easy boil, a few notches above mere simmer. The exact time depends on the age of the beans. Older beans require a longer period. Check the beans for saltiness, adding whatever is necessary to taste. The bean is done when it turns to cream between the teeth. Serve with any kind of sausage and ditto with bread, from corn muffin to crusty French chunk, with a side dish of chow-chow and generous slice of Vidalia onion.

Set a place for me.

TOM SAVINI'S
STIR FRIED VEGETABLES

What you will always find in my fridge are lots of fresh vegetables. I am not a vegetarian, but fill up daily on lots of them. I spray a no calorie, non fat butter spray into a frying pan, and put lots of sliced mushrooms, broccoli, cabbage, green beans, cauliflower, tomato, and stir fry them, and then add Braggs liquid amino acid, which is like a soy sauce, only healthier. The veggies come out nice and crisp and partly cooked and the texture is a lot nicer than steamed, and it is so good that I am going to make some now.

SELECTED GENRE FILMOGRAPHY

TOM SAVINI (1946-)

TV:

Director:
Tales From the Darkside (1984)

FEATURES:

Special effects:
Dead of Night (1974)

Martin (1977)

Dawn of the Dead (1978)

Creepshow (1982)

Creepshow 2 (1987)

Two Evil Eyes (1990)

Make-up:
Friday the 13th (1980)

Day of the Dead (1985)

The Texas Chainsaw Massacre 2 (1986)

Monkey Shines (1988)

Trauma (1993)

Necronomicon (1994)

Actor:
Dawn of the Dead (1978)

Creepshow (1982)

Two Evil Eyes (1990)

Innocent Blood (1992)

From Dusk Till Dawn (1996)

Dawn of the Dead (2004)

Land of the Dead (2005)

Director:
Night of the Living Dead (1990)

The Forest (2007)

MIXED VEGETABLES INDIAN STYLE

INGREDIENTS

4	tablespoons butter	½	teaspoon ground pepper
1	onion sliced	½	cups sliced green beans
1	clove garlic minced	¾	cup sliced carrots
2	teaspoons ground coriander		Water
1	teaspoon ground cumin	¾	cup peas, fresh or frozen
1	teaspoon chili powder		

DIRECTIONS

Melt butter in a heavy pan and add onion and garlic. Cook over low heat until translucent. Add spices and cook for a few minutes stirring constantly. Add carrots and beans and stir until mixed. Add enough water to cover vegetables and bring to a boil. Lower heat and simmer 10 to 15 minutes. Add peas during last 5 minutes. Add more water if necessary.

"GIMME SOME ONIONS WILL YOU SALLY? THE WAY DAN'S PILING THEM ON, I'M GOING TO HAVE TO EAT SOME IN SELF DEFENSE."

STEVE MARCH (JOHN AGAR) TO SALLY FALLON (JOYCE MEADOWS).

THE BRAIN FROM PLANET AROUS (1957)

"EVERYTHING INSIDE IS EATABLE, I MEAN EDIBLE, I MEAN YOU CAN EAT EVERYTHING."

- WILLY WONKA (GENE WILDER)

WILLY WONKA & THE CHOCOLATE FACTORY (1971)

MEAL MOVIE SPOTLIGHT!

Exterminating Angel (1962)

Guests sit down to a Maltese Stew served with liver, honey and almonds only to find themselves unable to leave the opulent mansion. They spend the days fighting for any food and water they can find and are finally reduced to basic animal instincts in another brilliant satire from master Luis Bunuel.

ROD SERLING'S
GERMAN POTATO PANCAKES

Born in Syracuse, New York, Serling was a dramatic writer before creating *The Twilight Zone* and *Night Gallery*. Serling also co-wrote the script for *Planet of the Apes (1968)* and taught writing at Ithica College, New York. Serling, who passed away in 1975, once said, "Hollywood's a great place to live… if you're a grapefruit."

INGREDIENTS

1½	cups flour	1¾	cups milk
½	teaspoon. salt	2	teaspoons baking powder
1	tablespoon sugar	½	teaspoon baking soda
3	eggs	1	cup mashed potato

DIRECTIONS

Make a well in a large bowl out of flour, salt, baking soda and baking powder. Add milk and beaten eggs and stir in mashed potatoes. Beat ingredients in bowl until the batter is very thin, with no lumps.

Cook in a skillet or large frying pan on medium heat. Brush a bit of butter on pancakes as they begin to bubble. Then turn and cook until golden brown. Remove from heat and cut pancakes into quarters or desired size, then stack pancakes on a separate plate until served. Season with pepper if so desired.

Makes: about 10 pancakes

Rod served these pancakes with his barbecued steaks.

"YOU KNOW MYRA, SOME PEOPLE MIGHT THINK YOU'RE CUTE. BUT ME? I THINK YOU'RE ONE VERY LARGE BAKED POTATO."

- MACHINE GUN JOE VITERBO
(SYLVESTER STALLONE)
DEATH RACE 2000 (1975)

ROBERT J. SERLING ...ON ROD SERLING

Older brother of Rod Serling, who was technical advisor on a couple of original *Twilight Zone* episodes, including "The Odyssey of Flight 33." He appeared in a documentary from the PBS American Masters series, entitled *Rod Serling: Submitted For Your Approval (1995)*. Serling, a novelist who specializes in aviation, continues to write in the western USA.

Potato pancakes was Rod's sole contribution to the culinary arts. I do remember they were delicious. Rod carried the formula around in his head. Rod did an expert job of barbecuing on an outdoors grill, although I doubt whether this skill would qualify him for any honor roll of Great Chefs.

Carol Serling called me and confirmed other than his ability to cook steaks and hamburgers on a grill, the potato pancakes constituted his only culinary skill. Rod's habit of putting ketchup on ice cream is another matter entirely — and absolutely true.

SET FOOD HORROR!

The food served on movies isn't all that it's cracked up to be. Here are some contributors with their own take on the situation.

"The lunch wagon is always horrifying. I bring my own!"
— P.J. Soles

"Studio commissary meals ain't that good; you suffer..."
— Allain Caillou

"Bruised bananas."
— John Zacherle

"Whatever the commissary was serving — except stew."
- Kate Phillips

KATE PHILIPS'S
BRANDIED YAMS

Kate Philips started her career as an actress working on broadway before getting roles in classic movies of the 1930's and 40's such as *Young Mr. Lincoln* and *Laura*. She turned to writing after meeting her husband and wrote *The Blob*. She currently teaches her craft at college.

I believe it was Thanksgiving of 1922 when our cook, Roxy came to my mother "Ma'am, the sweet potatoes are no good." My mother went with her to the kitchen saying, "Don't worry. I'm sure we can fix that." But when she tasted the golden, smoothly mashed yams she agreed.

"You're right, Roxy. No flavor."

"What we going to do, Ma'am?"

"Bring me the brandy decanter from the dining room," Mother said after a moment's thought.

Roxy did as she was told and mother took the crystal decanter, took off the crystal stopper and splashed brandy into the yams. She tasted the result, then added more brandy. After several "applications," she nodded. Then she gave Roxy a taste. Roxy nodded. Mother said, "Put it in a buttered casserole, cover with marshmallows and pop it in the oven."

"Yes, Ma'am," Roxy smiled. "We've made us a nice dish: brandied yams." And that's how you do it.

Add brandy to mashed sweet potatoes until you can taste the brandy. Then cover with marshmallows. Years later a friend of mine commented, "Delicious! First time I ever got drunk on sweet potatoes!"

"THE GIRL OF MY DREAMS IS A VEGETABLE!"
- CHAD FINLETTER
RETURN OF THE KILLER TOMATOES! (1988)

SELECTED GENRE FILMOGRAPHY

KATE PHILLIPS aka KAY LINAKER (1913-)

FILM

Actor:
The Invisible Woman (1940)

Screenwriter:
The Blob (1958)

The Blob (1988)

TED V. MIKELS'S
VEGGIE POT

Known by his trademark handlebar moustache, Mikels is practically a one man film studio having written, produced, acted, edited, directed and performed his own stunts. He began his career doing camera work for other film-makers and graduated to making his own. He has over 50 years and 100 film credits to his name. He has 6 kids, 25 grandchildren and 8 great-grandchildren and lives in Las Vegas Nevada where he still makes movies — his way.

INGREDIENTS

1	eggplant, chopped and peeled into 1 inch squares	1	can stewed tomatoes
1	cabbage		Garlic
2	carrots		Salt and pepper
1	cauliflower		Apple cider vinegar
3	brussel sprouts		

DIRECTIONS

Put eggplant into a steamer-pan (or waterless cookware). Cut chunks of cabbage into pieces an inch or two long. Chop carrots into one inch long pieces at an angle. Cut a cauliflower into one-inch pieces. Sometimes a few brussel sprouts cut in two add a great flavor. Add the stewed tomatoes, sliced in large pieces or into halves. Add several chopped-up pieces of peeled garlic. Add salt and pepper to taste, then, add enough vinegar to give the steamed and soft veggie pan a bitey-tangy taste. Serve the dish in bowls.

With a piece of the protein meat of your choice, you have a complete nourishing meal. I LOVE IT, it tickles my palette.

"YOU MADE A MESS OF YOURSELF! SPINACH IS FOR RABBITS, PEOPLE AND POPEYE, NOT ROBO-BOYS."

- LAB TECHNICIAN TO DAVID
(HALEY JOEL OSMENT)
A.I: ARTIFICIAL INTELLIGENCE (2001)

PAT PRIEST'S
CHILIS RELLENO CASSEROLE

Born in Utah, Priest took over for Beverley Owen as Marilyn on the hit comedy show, *The Munsters* which ran for two seasons. Priest also appeared in television shows *My Favorite Martian* (1964) and *Voyage to the Bottom of the Sea* and the cult classic movie *The Incredible 2-Headed Transplant* (1971).

INGREDIENTS

1	pound Jack Cheese	1	can (7 ounce) whole Ortega green chilies
1	pound Cheddar cheese	1	can (8 ounce.) tomato sauce
1	can (7 ounce) green chili salsa	2	cans evaporated milk
		4	eggs

DIRECTIONS

Wash the green chilies, remove seeds and lay them flat in a 9x12 pan. Grate cheese and put on top.

In a mixing bowl, beat eggs and milk and pour over cheese. Bake for 30 minutes in 350°F oven. Mix tomato sauce and salsa and pour over casserole. Cover and bake for 20 more minutes. Let stand for 10 minutes before serving.

"LOOK MARGARET HOW THEY DEVOUR THOSE CHUNKS OF MEAT! THESE CARNIVOROUS PLANTS ARE REMARKABLY CONSTRUCTIVE. THEIR STRONG STEMS SECRETE AN ACID ENZYME THAT DIGESTS ALMOST ANYTHING."

- DR. CHARLES DECKER (MICHAEL GOUGH)

KONGA (1961)

RICHARD HATCH'S
VEGETABLE CASSEROLE

Richard Hatch began his career in television and is best known for his work on *The Streets of San Francisco*, and *Battlestar Galactica*. He has since been seen in the new version of the show on the Sci-fi network *Battlestar Galactica*.

INGREDIENTS

2 - 3	cups penne noodles (or use your favorite pasta)	4	tomatoes sliced
1	cup Cheddar cheese or Jack cheese, grated	1	tablespoon garlic powder
3	cups fresh mixed vegetables, chopped (carrots, broccoli, cauliflower, celery)	1	tablespoon lemon juice
		2	tablespoons soy sauce or Liquid Aminos
1	cup cabbage or spinach leaves, chopped	1	tablespoon Spike seasoning
		1	cup whole grain brown rice (or basmati)

DIRECTIONS

Cook rice, and noodles according to package directions. They should be firm and crisp (al dente) Add soy sauce to the mixed vegetables.

Layer the bottom of a casserole dish with the rice. Place a layer of cabbage or spinach leaves over the rice. Add the vegetables on top of the cabbage. Add a layer of cabbage and spinach. Sprinkle spike and garlic powder over the leaves. Place the noodles over the cabbage leaves. Add the sliced tomatoes and another sprinkle of spike and garlic powder. Add a layer of the grated cheese.

Place in oven at 325°F for one hour or until top is really well browned. It will be bubbling. It mixes well together and is absolutely delicious.

Optional: You can add a layer of cooked beef, chicken or fish if you like.

STUFFED PEPPERS

INGREDIENTS

4	green peppers	1	yellow pepper, diced
½	pound sliced mushrooms	3	cloves garlic, minced
		½	cup bread crumbs
1	red onion, diced	3	teaspoons fresh basil, chopped
2	diced zucchini, green and yellow	1	tablespoon olive oil
1	red pepper, diced	Salt and Pepper	

DIRECTIONS

Slice the top off the green peppers and remove the seeds.

Parboil the green peppers for 5 minutes.

Saute mushrooms, onions and the red and yellow peppers in the olive oil until soft.

Add the garlic, salt and pepper. Saute for an additional three minutes or until garlic is soft. Remove from heat. Add the basil and bread crumbs.

Fill the green peppers and replace top. Bake for 15 minutes at 350ºF.

"THESE AREN'T REAL ONIONS, ARE THEY? THEY'RE SOME KIND OF ALIEN YUCKO ONIONS. WONDER IF THIS IS REAL CHEESE?"

- PETER (DAVID MENDENHALL)
SPACE RAIDERS (1983)

MEAL MOVIE SPOTLIGHT!

Little Shop of Horrors (1960)

Jack Nicholson makes one of his first appearances in this horror comedy shot in three days from Roger Corman. Jonathan Haze plays plant store cleark Seymour Krelboyne who nurses a bloodthirsty plant that feeds on people in order to grow. It became the basis for a broadway musical which was remade with Rick Moranis in 1986.

LLOYD KAUFMAN
...ON USEFUL INGREDIENTS

New York City native Kaufman, began his career working in various capacities on such films as John Badham's *Saturday Night Fever* and *Rocky*. He founded Troma Studios and wrote, produced and directed dozens of "science gone wrong" low-budget genre movies. Some of Kaufman's most memorable collaborations include *The Toxic Avenger, Class of Nuke 'Em High* and most recently, *Poultrygeist: Night of the Chicken Dead.*

The following is an excerpt from his book *All I Need To Know About Filmmaking I Learned From The Toxic Avenger.*

CANTALOUPE

In *The Toxic Avenger*, the head was nothing more than a simple cantaloupe. There was no face mold or latex skin. We merely rigged a child's body and put a cantaloupe loaded with cranberry sauce at the top of it. When the tire crosses over it, it created a splatterific sight. As with all special effects, editing is an important part of the magic. You can't let the camera linger for too long lest the audience sees it is not a squashed head but common produce."

© *Troma Entertainment. Reprinted with permission of the author.*

"COME AND GET IT! IT'S A RUNNING BUFFET! ALL YOU CAN EAT!"
- SHAUN (SIMON PEGG) TAUNTING FLESH EATING ZOMBIES.
SHAUN OF THE DEAD (2004)

THE BERT I. GORDON HOUSEHOLD

BY SUSAN GORDON

Bert I. Gordon is known in Hollywood as "Mr. Big" for his giant creature-feature films of the 1950's and beyond. Titles like *Beginning of the End*, *Attack of the Puppet People*, and *King Dinosaur* with special effects work shared by his wife Flora. Father of Susan Gordon, who appeared in some of his films, including *Picture Mommy Dead (1966)*. Gordon is now retired, but recently attended the Monster Bash convention in 2006.

Like in most any other household, food played an important part in the Gordon family traditions. There were always those special dishes that mom made, Treats we could look forward to on birthdays, holidays, and other special occasions. In the fall, when the Italian plums were in season, there was mom's plum cake. Dad would bring home literally a bushel or two of plums, and my two sisters and I would spend several days in the kitchen with mom, baking an endless number of plum cakes. They were then wrapped up and frozen, ready to be thawed on another day when we would have company over, or when we'd go to someone's house for a party and needed to bring something. It was always plum cake, and mom was well known for hers.

There were other favorite recipes that were part of our family lore, like the chocolate chip "blondies" and the corn-flake-crumb oven-fried chicken mom always brought up to us on visitor's day at sleep-away camp, or the chocolate angel food cake topped with chocolate whipped cream that she made for us on birthdays, and the "s'mores" we made over the open campfire when camping out. The s'mores (toasted marshmallows sandwiched in with a piece of chocolate bar between two graham crackers) probably were named that because they were so good, you'd definitely want "some more."

Then there was my grandmother's raspberry and whipped cream Jello mold at Thanksgiving, her homemade blintzes with sour cream, and her indescribably delicious apple turnovers, which I later discovered were really made by Pepperidge Farm!

After a while, it didn't matter that grandma hadn't really made them. In the end, I realized that it wasn't so much the food or the recipe as it was the love behind it that made it special.

Now, years later, I have a family of my own, and some of the same recipes I grew up on have become favorites among my children, as well. A tradition passed down.

A new favorite in our household is this delicious vegetable and sweet rice dish (page 69), so easy to make and so satisfying. It's especially nice on a cold winter's day, for it warms the body while it nourishes the soul. I hope you enjoy it!

Photo above is Susan with her father Bert on the set of Tormented (1960).

LISA WILCOX
THE GREEN TEETH

Lisa played the lead in *A Nightmare on Elm Street 4: The Dream Master* and the following sequel. She is known to Star Trek fans as Yuta in an episode of *Star Trek: The Next Generation* and *Watchers Reborn* opposite Mark Hamill. She has received international acclaim creating jewelry for her current endeavor Toe Brights.

I guest starred on *Star Trek, The Next Generation* as Yuta in "The Vengeance Factor." Captain Rikker (Jonathan Frakes) and I were falling in love but in the end he had to kill me. Anyway, I was the sovereign's cook and servant and the Captain wanted to try one of my dishes, an Acamarian dish called "Parthus," as he named "Parthus a la Yuta."

Well, we were filming as he dipped into this meal and "cut" was called.

The prop folks had used green food coloring to make this dish and it completely stained his teeth. He tried brushing with toothpaste but that did not work. Finally, an hour later, someone showed up with peroxide which Jonathan rinsed his mouth in and finally, his nice white teeth had returned and we were back to filming the scene. I felt so bad for him!

WALTER PHELAN
...ON EATING WITH MAKE-UP

Phelan was perfectly cast as Dr. Satan in *The House of 1000 Corpses* and has appeared in other horror shows in astonishingly grisly make-up, including *Wishmaster* and a recent television episode of *Masters of Horror,* "The Fair-Haired Child" (2006). Phelan keeps busy with film conventions and acting.

Sometimes I can't eat due to the make-up I wear. If I can get a slice or slit in the rubber over my mouth I can eat things like carrot sticks or celery or those bread sticks that are dipped in chocolate or strawberry.

Sometimes if I'm wearing a full body suit, you don't want to eat too much because it's so tight and so much physical work, you could feel bad if you have eaten.

MAKEUP TROUBLE!

"They told me earlier in the day that with the ape mask for my guest star orangutan role as Bandor, one couldn't eat through the costume at all. So I had to drink a bite to eat. All day long I could sip on a milkshake, and eat no solid food. The darn costume was on and was the most miserable thing. I almost gave up being an actor!" – Jay Robinson on working in *The Planet of the Apes (1968)*

"During filming of the *Planet of the Apes* series, I was usually famished by lunchtime but could only have something through a straw because of my heavy makeup."

– Booth Colman

The Wizard of Oz (1939)
The cowardly lion's facial makeup involved wearing a brown paper bag over his face. Actor Bert Lahr couldn't eat without ripping it. Tired of eating soup and milkshakes, he decided to eat lunch and have his makeup redone instead.

"Eating was impossible when I did *Planet of the Apes*. We drank our lunch out of a long straw."

- Beverly Garland

WHAT'S EATING YOU?
The Vegetables

Attack of the Killer Tomatoes (1978) – Killer tomatoes attack in this notorious bad horror movie spoof.

Attack of the Mushroom people (1963) – Survivors from a ship wreck end up on a deserted tropical island where they succumb to a deadly fungus that turns them into mushroom people.

The Woman Eater (1958) – A mad scientist feeds woman to his flesh-eating plant which then gives him a serum that helps bring the dead back to life.

Invasion of the Body Snatchers (1956, 1978) – The world is overcome by plant people who hatch from giant pods.

The Day of the Triffids (1962) – After a meteor shower leaves all those who view it blind, killer plants rise up and take over England. Adapted from the novel by John Wyndham.

Little Shop of Horrors (1960, 1989) – This early Roger Corman produced low budget movie about a killer plant and his owner was filmed in a few days. It became a cult hit and spawned a popular stage musical version that was filmed in the 80's with Rick Moranis and Steve Martin in the role originated by Jack Nicholson in the original.

Island of the Doomed (1967) – A giant blood sucking tree uses its branches to grab an unsuspecting victim.

The Navy vs. the Night Monsters (1966) – A scientific expedition to Antarctica discovers mysterious dormant plant specimens that grow up to be nocturnal tree monsters that secrete acid.

Poltergeist (1982) – A poltergeist fashions a kid eating tree in the backyard of a family house.

The Mutations (1974) – A scientist (Donald Pleasance) experiments with crossing animals with plants. A victim becomes a man eating plant and eats a drunk caught in the wrong place at the wrong time.

The Thing from Another World (1951) – Scientists discover a spacecraft buried beneath the ice in the Arctic in this moody atmospheric chiller produced by Howard Hawks. The frozen body of the pilot is found out to be "a giant carrot." It is accidentally thawed, it goes on a killing rampage.

Swamp Thing (1982) – A fighting vegetable movie but this time he's the good guy. When Dr. Alec Holland tries to combine animal and plant DNA things go horribly wrong and a new half plant, half man, all superhero is born.

Minority Report (2002) – A poisonous plant nearly kills Tom Cruise. He survives.

PASTA

AL LEWIS'S
GRAMPA'S FETTUCCINI WITH ROASTED GARLIC

New York City born, Lewis earned a PhD in child psychology from Columbia. He turned to acting and was lured by the television boom of fifties. He first came to attention with *Car 54, Where Are You?* but is best remembered as "Grandpa Munster" on the long running horror spoof *The Munsters*. Lewis appeared in numerous TV shows including *Lost in Space* and *Night Gallery*. Lewis had a restaurant in Greenwich Village called "Grampa's."

INGREDIENTS

Tomatoes

Artichokes

3	tablespoons olive oil
1	heated garlic
1	small onion, sliced thin
6	plum tomatoes seeded and chopped
½	pound spinach fettuccini

1	jar artichoke hearts drained and chopped
½	cup vegetable stock
1	tablespoon fresh thyme, chopped

Parmesan or Romano cheese, grated

Salt and pepper

DIRECTIONS

Preheat oven to 350ºF. Chop the tip off garlic head to expose cloves; pull off loose peel. Drizzle with one tablespoon of olive oil. Sprinkle with fresh pepper. Bake in foil for 5 minutes. Prepare the rest as garlic bakes.

Add fettuccini to pot of boiling water. Cook for 8-12 min. or until tender. Drain.

Add remaining two tablespoons of olive oil to large skillet and heat. Sauté onion until wilted. Mix in tomatoes, artichokes and thyme; sauté for 5 minutes. Stir in veggie stock and bring to a boil. Add pasta and heat through at high temperature for 2 min. Squeeze garlic head to release cloves; stir into mixture. Season to taste. Top with cheese.

Gramps says if you eat this dish 3 times a week, you'll live to be at least 87.

ANDREW FLEMING'S
PASTA LIMONE

Andrew Fleming graduated from New York University film school. He began his career making the low budget slasher *Deadly Friend*. He directed the critically acclaimed comedy-drama *Threesome* before casting a success spell on the box office with *The Craft*. The comedies *Dick* and the remake of Arthur Hiller's *The In-Laws* followed.

INGREDIENTS

- 1 pound high quality dry Italian tagliatelle or fettuccini
- Zest of 3 Lemons, finely shredded
- 1 Lemon, juice only
- 1 cup whole cream or maybe a little more
- 1 egg yolk
- Parmesan cheese, preferably Parmagiano Reggiano
- Italian parsley, chopped
- Salt and pepper

DIRECTIONS

Cook the pasta in abundant, generously salted water. Make sure not to overcook; Al dente is really best.

Meanwhile, beat the egg yolk into the cream and heat this up in a saucepan over low heat, stirring frequently, until it thickens just slightly. Add the lemon zest, juice and the cheese to the cream mixture, stir and remove from heat.

Salt and Pepper. If it's too thick, add a little more cream. It shouldn't be thick, like an Alfredo Sauce.

When the pasta is done, drain and toss, with the sauce lightly. Serve immediately with a sprinkle of parsley and maybe some more cheese.

"LET'S JUST CHEW OUR WAY OUT OF HERE."
- JACK BURTON (KURT RUSSELL)
BIG TROUBLE IN LITTLE CHINA (1986)

SELECTED GENRE FILMOGRAPHY

ANDREW FLEMING

TV:

The Witching Hour (Himself) (1996)

Producer
Paranormal Girl (2002)

FEATURES:

Writer-Director:
Bad Dreams (1988)

The Craft (1996)

DANIEL RICHTER'S
PASTA DEVRA

Daniel Richter was an assistant to John Lennon and took the photo on the cover of his first solo record. He played "Moonwatcher" from *2001: A Space Odyssey,* the early man who threw the bone in the air at the end of the opening "Dawn of Man" sequence. He played a vital role in choreographing the ape movement. He authored the book *Moonwatcher's Memoir A Diary of 2001: A Space Odyssey* on his experiences working on the film

INGREDIENTS

1	pound penne	½	cup of roughly chopped fresh basil
½	cup of extra virgin olive oil	¼	cup of sliced black olives
1	cup sun dried tomatoes	1-2	quartered lemons
4-5	cloves of garlic		Salt and pepper
6	chopped scallions		Parmesan cheese

DIRECTIONS

Blanch, dry and slice the dried tomatoes and set aside in some of the oil. Cook the penne and set it aside. Do not overcook the penne as it must be al dente. Heat the remaining olive oil in a large skillet and add the garlic. Soften the garlic but do not brown. Add the dried tomatoes and their oil. Let them cook for a minute or 2 to come up to heat and add the penne. Add the scallions, basil and olives. Salt and pepper to taste and place in a serving dish. Squeeze the lemons over the penne and add them to the final presentation. Garnish with the Parmesan cheese.

MEAL MOVIE SPOTLIGHT!

The Discreet Charm of the Bourgeoisie (1972)

Luis Bunuel's masterpiece follows a group of upper class friends who never manage to finish a meal together due to increasingly surreal interruptions. A restaurant funeral, attacking army guerrillas and an unexpected turn as reluctant participants in a play among other wonderful touches highlight the work of a film-maker at the top of his form.

JOHN AGAR'S
TAGLIARINI

Agar is best known to sci-fi fans for his work in many 1950's cult favorites like *The Brain from Planet Arous*, *Tarantula*, *Revenge of the Creature*, *The Mole People* and *Attack of the Puppet People*. Agar never fully retired from Hollywood and his last film, *The Naked Monster*, was released three years after his passing.

INGREDIENTS

1	package noodles	2	small cans tomato sauce
1	can cream corn	1½	pound ground beef
1	medium onion chopped	1	tablespoon chili powder
1	small can chopped olives	½	teaspoon salt
1	cup Cheddar cheese grated		

DIRECTIONS

Cook noodles and drain.

Brown ground beef.

Combine all ingredients in a casserole dish. Save some Cheddar cheese for the top of the casserole. Bake for 30 or 40 minutes at 350°F.

BATS!

The only food story on a movie that comes to mind is *Golden Mistress* filmed in Haiti. The food was terrible! The hotel packed our lunches which we took on location. They consisted of warm, soggy chicken sandwiches which we ate because we were starving. Our evening dinner was spoiled because the power failed and they lit candles at every table. Being hot, all the windows were open and lo and behold all the bats flew in. Needless to say it was very hectic, especially for the women to keep the bats out of their hair.

LENI PARKER'S
PASTA AL PESTO

New Brunswick born and raised Leni Parker graduated from Concordia University with a Bachelor of Fine Arts in Performance. From there she spent 10 years with the Pigeon International Theatre, a stint that took her to many countries. She moved on to notable film roles in Christian Duguay's *Screamers* and Deny Arcand's *Stardom*. She has developed a devoted fan following thanks to her role as Da'an in *Gene Roddenberry's: Earth: Final Conflict.*

INGREDIENTS

2	teaspoons salt	⅓	cup pesto sauce, store bought or make your own
3	tablespoons olive oil		
½	pound small red potatoes	½	cup soy cream
¼	pound green beans, cut in 1 inch pieces	½	pound dried penne pasta
			salt and pepper
2	cloves garlic, crushed		

DIRECTIONS

Bring water to boil with the salt and one tablespoon of the oil. Parboil the cut green beans for 2 minutes and then let cool on a plate. Place the potatoes in the boiling pot and cook for 10 to 15 minutes until tender. Drain and cut into ¼ inch thick pieces. Heat a frying pan and add two tablespoons of the oil and garlic. Add the potatoes and green beans. Sauté for 5 minutes until veggies are tender. Mix the pesto sauce with the soy cream and set aside. Boil the pasta until al dente. Drain and return to pot. Add the sautéed beans, potatoes, pesto and the soy cream. Toss together and add salt. Sprinkle with Parmesan if desired.

TAG LINES!

"A DELICIOUS ODYSSEY INTO THE BUCKET OF MADNESS"

POPCORN! (2001)

"A TASTY HORROR FILM!"

THE MEATEATER (1979)

MARK VERHEIDEN'S
LUCKLESS WRITER'S MACARONI & CHEESE

A long time comic book and movie fan, Mark Verheiden studied film-making at Portland State University. Hoping to break into screen-writing, he ended up with a stint writing for the Los Angeles Times. He wrote comic books and graphic novels like *Predator*, *Aliens* and *Timecop* and eventually got his wish to write for movies and television.

Most starving writers have tales of surviving on generic, boxed macaroni and cheese; the stuff was always cheap and relatively efficient, but waste-wise the cardboard box was probably more flavorful. Additionally, there was always something suspect about those envelopes of yellow cheese powder, especially when it clumped together. Did you ever bite into one of those powdery clumps? It was like no cheese I'd ever tasted!

So even in poverty, I was determined to avoid the boxed macaroni stigma. Unfortunately, I was still "in poverty," which meant my culinary means were restricted. But I think I came up with a substitute that was almost as cost efficient, and tastier to boot.

INGREDIENTS

Bag of macaroni noodles
1   can Campbell's Cheddar Cheese soup
1   can tuna fish, (optional)

DIRECTIONS

Bring a 2 quart saucepan of water to a boil. Throw in the entire bag of noodles and let boil for 20 minutes. Stir occasionally to prevent sticking; reduce heat if the pan boils over.

Drain noodles. Add can of soup. Stir. Add tuna if feeling frisky. Stir and serve.

Delicious home-made cooking, with heaps of leftovers, and at a price even the most luckless writer could afford.

FAVORITE FOOD:

Punctured Neck of Spring Femme, Assorted Deadly Fungi and a nightshade salad with Hemlock Dressing, naturally!

FAVORITE DRINK:

Bloody Mary. What else??

MICHAEL PATE'S
FETTUCCINI BUENA VISTA

Born in Sydney, New South Wales, Pate's first major horror role was as Drake Robey in *Curse of the Undead*. Pate starred opposite Vincent Price in *The Tower of London (1962)* and continues to write, produce and direct in his native Australia. Pate won critical accolades for writing, directing and producing the early Mel Gibson film Tim (1979)

Salsa de Pomodora

Blanch one pound of Italian Roma tomatoes, then skin, quarter, seed and dice. Squash (NOT cut, slice, shake or stir!) 3 large cloves of garlic and sauté in half a cup of olive oil until beginning to turn brown, then remove squashed cloves and discard. Add the tomatoes, and sauté for 3 minutes, then mix in sliced leaves of sweet basil, Italian parsley and oregano and set aside.

Mussels

Beard, scrub and rinse one kilogram (two pounds) of mussels.

In a lidded sauté pan, sauté two cupfuls of finely sliced celery, white onion and garlic until just turning opaque. Then add a grind or two of black peppercorns, a half cup of dry white wine and a half cup of stock — fish, preferably. Bring to the boil and then put the mussels in the pan, cover and allow to steam until they open.

Discard any that do not!

Fettuccini

Bring a pasta pot two-thirds full of well-salted water to the boil, put in the fettuccini and leave until a small piece tests as being al dente — this is, firm but starch-free to the taste when chewed. Do NOT add olive oil to the boiling water. Adding oil prevents the salsa from coating the fettuccini.

To Serve, pour the cooked fettuccini along with its water into a colander set in a skin. Vigorously shake any excess water from the fettuccini and deposit in a warmed serving bowl, preferably ceramic.

Douse the fettuccini with re-heated salsa de pomodora and mix thru. Remove the opened mussels and only the opened mussels! - from the pan in which they have steamed and shovel on top of the salsa-ed pasta, then place this Italian feast on the table and let the people help themselves with various servers you have provided — fettuccini forks, salsa scoopers, mussel manipulators — and go to it. Buano Appetito!

(N.B. — nota bene: Those of you with the instincts of vampires could, of course, substitute a quart of thickly-clotted human blood for the Salsa de Pomodora but that's up to the individual — and the obvious difficulty involved in laying your hands (and your fangs, most likely) on such a supply of gourmet blood!)

Curse of the Movie Marquee

In 1959, on the way to Australia with my wife, Felippa and my son, Christopher to visit with family and relatives, we had to fly United to Honolulu and then go on the same night on a Qantas Super Constellation to Sydney.

Arriving in Honolulu with some 10 hours to while away, we headed for the terrace of the Halekalani Hotel on which in 1955 I'd done some scenes in the Raoul Walsh-directed film *The Revolt of Mamie Stover*.

I organized us for some cool drinks on the terrace and then took my six year old son down onto Waikili Beach for a swim. On the sand, in the surf, as we walked along the beach, back on the terrace, I couldn't help noticing that person after person was stopping when they saw me, staring, pointing at me, whispering to each other and then walking away backwards.

Still looking at me with a look of total misbelief — if not sheer horror on their faces.

This went on happening all day and into the evening and it wasn't until we were in a taxi heading for the airport that night, I realized what was the matter with all these people.

As the taxi stopped at a set of traffic lights, there on the marquee of a cinema, in big lights was:

"CURSE OF THE UNDEAD"

STARRING

ERIC FLEMING, KATHLEEN CROWLEY, MICHAEL PATE

It had just opened the day before! And it's not every day you see a vampire around town!

So my advice is: if you won't want people to point at you, never star in a vampire picture.

For good measure, my favorite saying — and it applies just as well to vampires getting on in years as to anyone else — is one attributed to Bette Davis and it is:

"Old age is not for sissies!"

"EVERYTHING TASTES BETTER HERE. EVEN THE WATER IS SWEET"

- NORTHER WINSLOW (STEVE BUSCEMI)

BIG FISH (2003)

BEST PASTA SCENES

AI: Artificial Intelligence (2001)

In a spaghetti dinner scene, a dangling noodle breaks the ice between robot son and parents.

A Clockwork Orange (1971)

Alex (Malcolm McDowell) has dinner with a writer and falls face first into his drugged spaghetti.

Alien (1979)

One last meal before they sleep, the crew of the Nostromo eats spaghetti like food. Everything is fine until an Alien bursts from the chest of John Hurt.

Bladerunner (1982)

Deckard gets the call to work while eating noodles. "Tell him I'm eating."

Lemony Snicket's A Series of Unfortunate Events (2004)

Adopted children of Count Olaf (Jim Carrey) prepare pasta Puttanesca for him. He wanted roast beef.

PETER JURASIK'S
THE BABYLON 5 MINUTE SAUCE

Born in Queens, New York, Jurasik is best known by sci-fi fans for his portrayal of Londo Mollari in the hit TV series *Babylon 5*. Jurasik, whose first sci-fi film was *Tron,* is also well known as Sid the Snitch on the show Hill Street Blues. Jurasik has also appeared in TV episodes of *3rd Rock from the Sun* and *Sliders*.

It's a well known fact but worth repeating that after spending years and years on a space station like *Babylon 5*, members of every race and species get mighty tired of the standard menu of Tang, dried ice cream, and Irish stew out of a squeeze tube or even Centauri delicacies like Fresh Spoo or Hot Jala. Here's a little something that's easy and fast to prepare but is guaranteed to make anyone, even space-faring astronauts, feel like they're sitting down in a quiet piazza in Roma for a home cooked meal.

INGREDIENTS

- ¼ cup extra-virgin olive oil
- 1 garlic clove, peeled and minced
- 1 28-ounce can imported Italian tomatoes
- 4-5 fresh basil leaves
- Salt and black pepper
- 1 pound penne pasta

DIRECTIONS

Heat the extra-virgin olive oil in a deep skillet. Add the garlic and cook briefly until it releases its characteristic aroma. Pass the tomatoes, juice and all, through the coarse disk of a food mill directly into the skillet. No food mill? Just cut up, tear apart and generally smoosh up the tomatoes in the skillet; they'll turn into a sauce with a little heat and cooking time. Add the fresh basil leaves.

Cook over a moderately high heat until the sauce thickens approximately 20 minutes. Hey remember, way out on the outer rim of space five *Babylon 5* minutes equals about 20 earth minutes... anyway I couldn't call it *The Babylon 5 20 minute sauce* could I? While the sauce is heating, cook the pasta in abundant boiling salted water until al dente. Quickly drain and place in a large serving bowl with the tomato sauce. Drizzle a little extra-virgin olive oil over the pasta and mix well with your amazingly rich and fresh

sauce. Add salt, pepper and grated cheese to taste. Now, pour yourself a small glass of cheap Chianti and grab a seat by the window to watch the moon rise over Saturn. It makes for a lovely meal.

Just don't invite any Narns or Klingons!

Serves: 4 to 6

KAREN BLACK'S
LOW FAT PASTA MEAT SAUCE

Black rose to fame after appearing in *Easy Rider* and is remembered for her roles in classics like *Family Plot, Five Easy Pieces* and *Nashville*. Horror fans know her best for her myriad roles in *Trilogy of Terror*. Black, who also writes, continues to act in genre films like Fred Olen Ray's *Invisible Dad* and Rob Zombie's *House of 1000 Corpses*.

INGREDIENTS

½	pound lean ground beef	Red pepper chili seeds
¼	cup onion flakes	Salt and pepper
	Oregano	1 cup tomato sauce
	Marjoram	2 tomatoes, sliced
1	pound whole wheat spaghetti or penne	

DIRECTIONS

Brown beef in pan. Add onion flakes, oregano, marjoram and chili seeds, salt and pepper.

Add tomato sauce and tomato slices and let simmer 5 to 10 minutes until thickened.

Pour over cooked pasta and serve.

WILLIAM SCHALLERT'S
VEGETARIAN SPAGHETTI WITH EGGPLANT

William Schallert has appeared in hundreds of films and television shows. He played many roles in popular 1950's science fiction movies that he later got to parody in Joe Dante's *Matinee*. He is perhaps best known for his *Star Trek* role as Nilz Barris in the classic episode "The Trouble with Tribbles" and as Martin Lane on *The Patty Duke Show*.

Ingredients

Extra virgin olive oil (to keep eggplant moist)

4 large cans crushed tomatoes

3 jars garlic (thick sliced)

2 eggplants (peeled, then chopped into ½" squares)

3 tablespoon tomato paste

½ cup chopped parsley

Salt

Finely ground pepper

Directions

In a large pan, cover bottom with olive oil. Heat. Put in crushed tomatoes and garlic slices.

In a separate pan cover bottom with olive oil. Sauté egg plant squares until tender. Salt to taste.

In large pan, add eggplant to tomato and garlic mixture. Add tomato paste, parsley, and pepper (don't overdo).

Simmer about 2 hours until sauce thickens.

Cook required amount of spaghetti until al dente. Cover with sauce. Top with shredded or grated Parmesan cheese. Serve with garlic bread.

Sometime in the early 1970's I accepted an invitation to attend a Star Trek Convention called Equon.con, as near as I can recall. It occupied the entire Marriott Hotel at LAX. As I entered the lobby, I was confronted by a throng of Trekkies in various "alien" disguises, many of which featured waving antennae attached to skull caps, bringing to mind 'the Killer Bees' of *Saturday Night Live* fame.

While I was transfixed by this bizarre spectacle, the "aliens" began pointing in my general direction, shouting "NILZ BARIS! NILZ BARIS!" When I looked behind me to see who they were pointing at, they began shouting, "No, it's YOU! You're NILZ BARIS! from "Trouble with Tribbles!"

Like most actors who have guest-starred on countless TV shows, I almost never remember the names of the characters I play: too many jobs; too short an involvement with each show. But in this case, at least, some devoted Star Trek fans made sure that the unlikely name, "Nilz Baris," was permanently tattooed on my brain.

One should never underestimate the power of Trekkies over one's life.

"IT'S HUNGRY! IT HAS TO BE FED CONSTANTLY OR IT WILL REACH OUT ITS MAGNETIC ARM AND GRAB AT ANYTHING WITHIN ITS REACH AND KILL IT. IT'S MONSTROUS, STEWART, MONSTROUS. IT GROWS BIGGER AND BIGGER!"

– HOWARD DENKER
THE MAGNETIC MONSTER (1953)

PASTA TRIVIA

Alien (1979)

To create the android's entrails, the effects crew used pasta and glass marbles.

In the Mouth of Madness (1995)

The car keys that Julie Carmen swallows when Sam Neill is trying to escape from town were made out of pasta.

Toxic Avenger (1985)

When a dog is killed the crew trained a dog to slide across the floor on command and created entrails from painted spaghetti.

Raiders of the Lost Ark (1981)

While filming in Tunisia, nearly the entire cast and crew got sick on the local food, except one: Director Steven Spielberg. He has the bright idea of bringing endless amounts of canned spaghetti.

RACHEL TALALAY'S
NOODLES MARMADUKE

Producer-director Talalay made her feature directing debut with *Freddy's Dead: The Final Nightmare* after showing her stuff as a line producer on such films as John Waters's *Hairspray* and the third and fourth Freddy Krueger films. Talalay continues to direct in and around Hollywood, Canada and the UK.

DIRECTIONS

Brown one pound of ground beef. (or some tofu substitute).

Add onions and mushrooms and brown them as well.

Dump in some sherry.

Couple of pinches of dill weed.

Salt and pepper of course.

Separately, cook up some noodles. Follow the instructions on the noodle package – you know, dump them in boiling water and so on. Add olive oil to keep from them from sticking.

Then, mix the meat mixture and the noodles with sour cream.

Garnish with parsley, except I hate parsley because you have to dunk it in salt water for Passover and that represents tears of oppression and that always freaked me out, like red wine being the blood of Christ. But let's not get into that.

MEAL MOVIE SPOTLIGHT!

Bad Taste (1987)

Peter Jackson's first film is a far cry from the big budget fantasy *Lord of the Rings.* Shot on weekends over the course of four years the plot deals with Aliens who farm humans as the main ingredient for their intergalactic fast food chain "Crumb's Crunchy Delights".

SELECTED GENRE FILMOGRAPHY

RACHEL TALALAY

www.racheltalalay.com

TV:

Space Rangers (Producer) (1993)

Director:
Wolf Lake (2001)

The Dead Zone (2006)

Wind in the Willows (2006)

FEATURES:

Director-Writer:
Freddy's Dead: The Final Nightmare (1991)

Director:
Ghost in the Machine (1993)

Tank Girl (1995)

Producer:
A Nightmare on Elm Street 4: The Dream Master (1988)

The Borrowers (1997)

PUMPKIN RAVIOLI WITH WHITE SAUCE

INGREDIENTS

FILLING:

1   tablespoon olive oil

½   cup mushrooms, finely chopped

2   shallots, finely chopped

2   garlic cloves, finely chopped

1   can (2 cups) pumpkin puree

¾   cup Asiago cheese, grated plus additional for topping

½   cup mashed potato flakes

⅛   teaspoon nutmeg

SAUCE:

¼   cup butter

¼   cup flour

2   cups milk

1   sprig of rosemary

1   small onion

5   or 6 whole cloves

     Salt and pepper

Nutmeg

DIRECTIONS

It is best to make the ravioli ahead of time.

Add olive oil to a pan and cook onion, garlic and mushrooms over low heat, stirring until the onions are soft and translucent about 5 minutes. Allow to cool. Mix the pumpkin, cheese, nutmeg, potato flakes, sesame oil, salt and pepper in a mixing bowl. Add the onions, garlic and mushroom mixture and stir until well blended. Cover and place in fridge until well chilled at least 1 hour.

Place a pasta sheet on a non stick cookie sheet or lightly floured surface. Place a teaspoon of the filling every 2 inches on the sheet and brush water around the filling. Place another sheet on top and cut with a knife or pizza wheel into two inch squares. Press firmly to seal the edges. At this point the ravioli can be covered and placed in the fridge for use the next day.

Bring a large pot of salted water to a boil and drop the ravioli in the water. The ravioli should be cooked in batches of 6 to 10 to prevent sticking. Boil for 2-3 minutes or until they float to the top. With a slotted spoon, remove the ravioli and place on a plate to drain. Brush ravioli with olive oil to prevent sticking. Repeat until all the ravioli is cooked.

White Sauce

Melt the butter in a medium saucepan over low heat. When the butter starts to look foamy, add the flour and mix with a wire whisk until well blended. Stick the cloves in the small onion and drop in the pan with the milk. Cook over low heat 3 to 4 minutes, stirring constantly. Remove pan from heat and allow to cool.

In a medium saucepan, scald milk until it's almost about to boil. Return the saucepan with the flour mixture to medium-low heat. Add the milk and stir well with the whisk. Reduce the heat to low and simmer while stirring with the whisk. Add the rosemary sprig and continue stirring until the sauce thickens, 15 to 20 minutes. Remove the onion with cloves and add the salt, pepper and nutmeg. Pour the sauce over the ravioli.

Grate fresh Asiago cheese over top and serve.

Serves: 2-4

VIC MIZZY
...ON RESTAURANTS

Born in Brooklyn, New York, Vic Mizzy is best known for creating the classic theme music for *The Addams Family* TV show. Mizzy's unmistakable keyboard sound can also be heard on William Castle's *The Night Walker* and horror spoofs like *The Ghost and Mr. Chicken* with Don Knotts. Mizzy now resides in southern California.

When I eat food and restaurant psychologically I think of a good dry cleaning store that can clean my clothes after staining my suit. Incidentally, I love all food especially Italian but I can't eat in an Italian restaurant where the chef can't pronounce marinara, as in sauce.

SELECTED GENRE FILMOGRAPHY

VICTOR MIZZY (1922-)

TV:

The Addams Family (1964)

FEATURES:

The Night Walker (1965)

The Ghost and Mr. Chicken (1966)

The Spirit Is Willing (1967)

The Reluctant Astronaut (1967)

Halloween With the New Addams Family (1977)

The Munsters' Revenge (1981)

The Addams Family (1991)

Addams Family Values (1993)

Spine Tingler: The William Castle Story (2008) (as Himself)

SCREAM QUEEN SPINACH PAPPARDELLE

OUR PICK

INGREDIENTS

- 2 pounds of spinach pappardelle or fettucini
- 2 red onions diced
- 1 red pepper
- 1 yellow pepper
- ¼ pound shitake mushrooms, chopped, stems removed
- ¼ cup of olive oil
- 3 cloves garlic
- 1 teaspoon chili flakes
- 3-4 cups of spinach, shredded
- 3 tablespoons soy parmigiano-Reggiano cheese

DIRECTIONS

Heat oil in a pan. Add the onions and mushrooms, peppers and chili flakes, salt and pepper. Saute on low for 5 minutes until the onions are soft.

Cook pasta in boiling salted water.

Add pasta to pan and quickly add the spinach leaves.

Top with the lemon juice and cheese.

LINNEA QUIGLEY ...ON FOOD

Born in Davenport Iowa, Linnea Quigley got work in low budget movies. She broke through with her outrageous role in *Return of the Living Dead* and earned the mantle "Queen of the B's." She moved to Florida and still makes movies and convention appearances. She has written two books about her experiences in the business: *I'm Screaming as Fast as I Can* and *Chainsaw*.

I'm a vegan so no animals. Pasta, spinach, garlic to keep the vampires at bay.

Chuck La France a fan then friend was a meat eater. He talked to me and two years later, he's 100 pounds lighter, happier and a devoted animal rights man.

I never ate food we had to make in home-ec class so they got mad, but I said it was unhealthy so they couldn't argue with me.

MICHAEL LENNICK'S
DEEP SPACE PASTA

Author, filmmaker and historian Michael Lennick was born in Toronto shortly before the dawn of the Space Age, an era that provided excellent reasons for skipping school on launch days, and the impetus for the rest of his career. For twenty years Michael divided his time between writing and directing kids' shows and documentaries for television and creating visual effects for numerous film and television projects, including David Cronenberg's *Videodrome* and the TV series *War of the Worlds*.

As I write this, the Space Age is nearly 50 years old. That's fairly alarming to an old fart who clearly remembers the night that first Russian Sputnik beeped its way across an otherwise pristine North American sky. The spacecraft's eerie pulse could be picked up on any shortwave radio, and in those days there was a dad or two on every block equipped with such technology. Sputnik marked the dawning of an era that would see humans on the moon less than twelve years later. In the intervening decades we've built manned space stations, launched tourists into orbit, and begun designing vessels for our first missions to Mars. Space travel has finally become a very real option for all those with the yearning, and the price of a ticket. And yet, oddly enough, the food still sucks.

That's why I've chosen to share a recipe we employ frequently on our many space-oriented filming expeditions. It's relatively easy to prepare, unbelievably tasty, and as breathtaking in its multi-layered glory as the clouds girding Jupiter. Please memorize and destroy (through eating, natch) these top-secret specifications for the patent-pending Foolish Earthling Productions...

CONTINUED...

SELECTED GENRE FILMOGRAPHY

MICHAEL LENNICK

TV:

Visual Effects:
Earthquake in New York (1998)

The Adventures of Sinbad (1996)

Harrison Bergeron (1995)

War of the Worlds (1988)

My Secret Identity (1988)

Friday the 13th (1987)

Writer-Director-Producer:
2001 and Beyond (2001)

FEATURES:

Visual Effects:
Millennium (1989)

The Dead Zone (1983)

Videodrome (1983)

Murder by Phone (1982)

VIDEO:

Writer-Director-Producer:
Videodrome: Forging the New Flesh (2004)

Ingredients

1	19-ounce can tomato sauce	1	package (1/2 pound) wheat or spinach lasagna noodles
1	19-ounce can stewed tomatoes, Italian style	1	16-ounce whole (not skim) mozzarella cheese
1	13-ounce can tomato paste	1	16-ounce ricotta cheese (small curd cottage cheese also works in a pinch)
2	cups water		
1	dozen large white mushrooms, sliced fresh garlic cloves (I use several, and have fewer friends each year)	1	egg
		1	- 2 tablespoons each of pepper, oregano, sugar, Italian seasoning
		1	pound lean or extra-lean ground beef (optional)

Got all that stuff ready? Okay, here we go:

You'll begin with a great sauce. Feel free to go meaty or veggie for this step. Both work equally well. If you already have your own patented sauce recipe, go ahead and make up a batch. Or heat up a couple of jars of your favorite commercial brand. Odds are I'll never find out. Here's the version we like: It originated with my mom, and I've probably refined it a bit nearly every time I've made it (as did Mom.) Unlike some of our recent endeavors, this recipe is not Rocket Science. It's built to be messed with. I suggest following it as closely as comfortable the first time out, then altering it to suit your own taste and spice tolerance over future iterations.

Brown the meat in a large saucepan. For a perfectly delicious Deep Space Veggie Lasagna (you unrepentant hippie you) just leave out the meat and start right in on the sauce. Down here in the vast Foolish Earthling Command Bunker we tend to alternate between versions.

Add (or begin by heating in a large saucepan) the stewed tomatoes, tomato sauce, tomato paste, and as much water as seems reasonable to bring it all to a slow boil. It should at this stage begin to present a nice, thick-but-stirable, appropriately-sauce-like consistency. This can be a bit tricky to quantify (and is very much a matter of personal taste) but to paraphrase US Supreme Court Justice Potter Stewart's 1973 opinion, you'll know it when you see it. (He was actually referring to pornography at the time.)

Slowly stir in the pepper, oregano, sugar, Italian seasoning, and any other spice or flavor (crumbled bay leaf, sliced green peppers etc.) you find appropriate to the desired mood. Stir in as much fresh crushed or pressed garlic as you figure your company can handle. As suggested earlier, we go a bit nuts around here on the garlic. Coincidentally, it's getting harder and harder to find good help.

Stir in the sliced mushrooms and let this astonishingly-lifelike concoction simmer on low heat for a while. The longer you can allow these flavors to blend, the better. (This will be a truly great spaghetti sauce tomorrow but darn it all, we've got a lasagna to build today.)

Boil the lasagna noodles in lightly salted water until al dente (about 6-7 minutes.) When done, drain the noodles into a large colander. Rinse with cold water to remove the starch.

While the noodles are boiling, let's prep the diary ingredients. Grate the mozzarella cheese into a large bowl. If you're substituting small-curd cottage cheese for Ricotta, place it in a bowl and stir in one whole egg and a bit of pepper. This is a trick my mom came up with to get cottage cheese to resemble Ricotta, a very hard substance to find when I was a kid for some reason. We liked the results so much that to this day we alternate between Ricotta and the cottage cheese/egg thing, but please feel free to stick with the Ricotta. Not having shared this or any other part of my childhood has worked well for you so far; Why mess with that now?

Okay, let's line up our key ingredients – drained noodles, sauce, mozzarella cheese, Ricotta or cottage cheese – we're going for assembly-line configuration. The following scene may come to disturbingly resemble Lucy in the chocolate factory, but the results should be much tastier. You're about to build something wonderful.

Place the first layer of noodles on the bottom of a large casserole pan. Five noodles should cover the bottom wall to wall, and a bit of overlap at the edges wouldn't hurt. Ladle some sauce over the noodles, covering them in gloppy red glory. A light layer of shredded mozzarella cheese comes next, followed by another layer of edge-to-edge noodles. Top evenly with the Ricotta cheese, followed by another layer of sauce. (A pattern should be starting to emerge…) Crowning layers of noodles, sauce and the rest of your mozzarella fills the pan to the rim. If we've both done our jobs properly the result should be gorgeous, heavy as hell, and ready for the oven.

Bake for 20 to 30 minutes at 400°-425°F using both top and bottom burners. You're looking for a nice, bubbly, golden-brown crust.

Results should ideally be served with Caesar Salad, garlic bread and a nice Chianti. This version of the recipe will serve 6 to 8 — or you, until such time as you can force yourself to stop eating it. Refrigerate leftovers and re-heat in a warm oven 300-350°F.

One final step...

Since I promised you a Deep Space Lasagna, you'll need to get hold of either a really strong baggie or a sterile latex pouch. De-hydrate a single serving of baked-then-cooled lasagna and seal it into the pouch, applying all standard industry sterilization protocols. When it's time to eat, re-hydrate the sealed package using hot water from your spacecraft's on-board Hydration Delivery System (basically a stainless steel hose) or the nearest kettle. And as you sit there, straining to avoid sucking your lung through the egress tube while savoring a meal far better suited to a plate astride checkered tablecloth festooned with Chianti bottle candlesticks, consider that this is exactly how they still do it. It's how John Glenn ate aboard Friendship 7 in 1962, and again on the Space Shuttle in 1998. And yes, it still sucks, in every sense of the word. Next time, try slicing the mushrooms thinner.

MEAL MOVIE SPOTLIGHT!

Soylent Green (1973)

Adapted from the late sixties novel *Make Room! Make Room!* by Harry Harrison, this futuristic tale of overpopulation stars Charleton Heston who discovers the secret ingredient behind the mysterious food known to the populace as Soylent. The last line by Heston has become a catch phrase much like his last line from *Planet of the Apes.*

Delicatessen (1991)

In a post-apocolyptic society, food is so rare that it is actually used as currency. The residents of an apartment buiding above a butcher shop receive the occasional order of meat in this highly rated quirky fantasy directed by Jean-Pierre Jeunet and Marc Caro.

POULTRY

TED V. MIKELS'S
SEASONED CHICKEN BREAST

A favorite meat dish of mine is boneless, skinless chicken breasts cut length-wise in slices not more than a ½-inch thick. Lay them out on the cutting board, sprinkle amply with garlic powder, seasoning salt, pepper, salt, and ground oregano flakes, a few bits of dried parsley.

Heat the non-stick frying pan to allow a thin smooth coat of butter or margarine to cover the bottom. When the pan is heated sufficiently, lay the chicken slices gently, seasoned side down into the melted butter. Turn over every few minutes but do NOT FRY them. Just keep turning until all of the meat turns white.

When done this way, the chicken is beautifully flavored and very tender. You'll love this dish, and it's so simple to make.

Serve with veggie pot. (page 71)

FORREST J. ACKERMAN'S
GOURMET HEAVEN

Los Angeles born Forry Ackerman aka "Uncle Forry," is known to legions of fans as the man behind the *Famous Monsters of Filmland* magazine. Ackerman, along with his lifelong friends Ray Bradbury and Ray Harryhausen, have all carved their own unique niche in the Hollywood age. Forry continues to act and make convention appearances.

Beijing, capital city of China. And Cheng-du, pop. 10 million. Each of the ten days I was in these two huge metropolises I was treated to gourmet lunches and dinners. The last lunch had five soups as starters and twenty-two courses. The grand finale features seven soups and thirty-six courses, including:

Oriels' Eggs

Little Eels

Black Chicken

and

World Famous Peking Duck

I don't know what the other delicacies were but the last night in Beijing I went out on the street by myself and walked a mile amidst a million bicyclers to get the best meal of my stay in China:

A Hamburger
French Fries
Apple Pie
Black Coffee
and
An Ice Cream Cone
at
MCDONALDS!

ANNE FRANCIS'S
SIMPLE ROAST CHICKEN WITH PAPRIKA

DIRECTIONS

My favorite meal would probably be a simple roast chicken. Bake about 20 minutes to a pound at 350°F.

Sprinkle with paprika and garlic salt.

Stuff with a mixture of cooked brown and wild rice to which you have added fruit (fresh and/or dried), whatever seasoning you like and a bit of wine. You choose. That's the fun!

Make a salad. I would probably do a medley of greens with my homemade dressing of blended minced garlic, olive oil, lemon and fresh basil. Salt and pepper to taste.

I would toast some sunflower seeds in the skillet to sprinkle later over the stuffing.

Garlic melba: Fingers of sour dough bread dipped in garlic butter and popped into the oven at a low temperature. This can be done the day before if you're planning ahead, or use the counter oven broiler. You want it to come out nice and crisp and crunchy.

Obviously it is no secret that I love garlic! That's probably why the "Monster From the Id" never laid a paw on me!

KENNETH BRANAGH'S
CHICKEN WITH AVOCADO

Branagh joined the Royal Shakespeare Company at 23 where he got star billing in *Henry V* and *Romeo and Juliet*. He formed his own Renaissance Theatre Company and directed and starred in the film *Henry V* while still in his twenties. Branagh made a whole generation of new fans as a dandy professor in *Harry Potter and the Chamber of Secrets*.

INGREDIENTS

1	medium sized chicken, cooked and cut into strips when cold	1	tablespoons dry sherry
4	tablespoons butter	2	ripe peeled avocados
4	tablespoons flour		Juice of 1 lemon
1¼	cup milk	1	ounce grated Cheddar cheese
⅔	cup chicken stock		Salt
⅔	cup cream		Pepper

DIRECTIONS

Over a low heat, melt the butter in a saucepan; add the sieved flour, blend into a smooth paste and cook for 2 minutes.

Remove from the heat and gradually stir in the milk and chicken stock. Put back on the heat and while stirring constantly, bring the sauce to simmering point and cook very gently for 3 minutes.

Remove from the heat and add the cream, the chicken pieces and sherry.

Season with salt and pepper and lemon juice.

Halve and slice the avocados (having skinned them first) put in an ovenproof dish and sprinkle with lemon juice. Spoon over with chicken mixture. Sprinkle with grated cheese and bake in oven for 30 minutes at gas mark 6 or 400°F.

"WHAT'S THAT? CHICKEN?"

- DR. FLOYD (WILLIAM SYLVESTER)
PONDERING SPACE FOOD.

2001: A SPACE ODYSSEY (1968)

DICK DUROCK'S
A DIFFERENT KIND OF CHILI

INGREDIENTS

2   pounds ground
     turkey (lean)

2   cans Mexican style diced
     or stewed tomatoes

2   cans black beans rinsed
     well and drained

1   can whole sweet
     corn drained

1   package dry chili mix
     (I like Carol Shelby's)

     Garlic to taste

1   medium diced onion

     Salt and pepper
     if needed

DIRECTIONS

Brown and drain turkey and set aside. Sauté onions and garlic 3 to 4 minutes. Return turkey to pan and sauté 5 minutes more.

Add everything else (including chili mix) with one cup of water.

Cover and cook over low heat for minimum of half an hour. (longer is better)

Before serving add Masa (fine corn meal) from chili mix package to thicken if desired.

TAG LINES!

"DON'T COME BEFORE DINNER!"
TEENAGE FRANKENSTEIN (1957)

"THE PROSPECT OF BEING COOKED ALIVE
IS NOT AN ATTRACTIVE ONE!"
FIRST MAN INTO SPACE (1959)

"HIDEOUS BEYOND BELIEF, WITH
AN INHUMAN CRAVING!"
QUEEN OF BLOOD (1966)

EDGAR G. ULMER'S
GEBRATENC GANS MIT APFELN
(GOOSE WITH APPLE AND PRUNE STUFFING)

Born in Austria-Hungary (now the Czech Republic), Ulmer is best known for his directorial work with Karloff and Lugosi in *The Black Cat (1934)*. He is well regarded for his gritty low budget dramas such as *Detour* and *The Naked Dawn*. Ulmer also directed the cult classic *Bluebeard (1944)* starring John Carradine. His daughter Arianne appeared in his later science fiction films like *Beyond the Time Barrier*.

INGREDIENTS

10-12	pound goose	1	tablespoon beef lard
18 to 20	prunes	1	teaspoon salt
	Port Wine	1	tablespoon butter
8	tart green apples, peeled, cored and quartered	1	cup boiling water
		1	tablespoon flour

DIRECTIONS

Cover eighteen to twenty prunes in Port and soak overnight. Simmer them in the port for 20 minutes or until the pits can easily be removed. Stone the prunes and add eight apples peeled, cored and quartered (tart green apples preferred), and sugar to taste.

Wash and dry a ten to twelve pound goose and rub the cavity with one tablespoon suet or beef lard. Stuff the goose with the apple mixture and sew up the opening. Rub the bird with one teaspoon salt. Turn the skin of the neck backward, and secure it with a small skewer. Twist the wings, back and truss the thighs. Prick the bird well with a fork and place it on a rack in a roasting pan.

Spread one tablespoon butter over the breast, add one cup boiling water and baste the goose in a moderately hot oven 375°F allowing 20 minutes per pound, basting frequently. Turn the goose until it is light brown on all sides. Remove the threads and skewers and transfer to a serving platter. Pour off the surplus fat from the "juices" in the pan. Stir in one tablespoon flour and make gravy.

Serve with chestnut puree, rice, or sweet and sour red cabbage.

HONOR BLACKMAN'S FAVORITE
SPICY CHICKEN

Born in London England, Blackman starred in early episodes of *The Avengers* and was in *The Invisible Man* TV show. Blackman is best remembered as Pussy Galore in *Goldfinger*, but also played the alluring goddess Hera in *Jason and the Argonauts*. Most recently Blackman appeared in the British TV show *Dr. Terrible's House of Horrible*.

INGREDIENTS

12	chicken pieces.	1	teaspoon curry powder
¼	cup butter, melted	4	tablespoon German or whole grain mustard
½	cup liquid honey		Salt and pepper

DIRECTIONS

Combine ingredients and pour sauce over chicken pieces. Cook 45 minutes in moderate 350°F oven turning once. Serve with rice or noodles.

POULTRY SCENES

Harry Potter and the Philosopher's Stone (2001)

Affable ghost *Nearly Headless Nick* (John Cleese) pops out of a roast chicken at a school feast and demonstrates his moniker to shocked students.

Monty Python and the Holy Grail (1975)

How to tell if one is a witch: If she weighs the same as a duck, she's made of wood and therefore a witch.

Eraserhead (1977)

Small chickens, squirm and ooze black liquid in one of the strangest dinner sequences in cinema history.

Sleeper (1973)

"That's a big chicken." One of the stranger things Allen comes across in the future is a farmer walking a giant chicken.

Gremlins (1984)

Billy (Zach Galligan) feeds his unusual new pets leftover chicken... after midnight.

ROBERT PICARDO'S
PIGEON DI STOOLO MORTO
(DEAD STOOL PIGEON IN BLOODY POOL WITH SEVERED TONGUE AND BULLET CASINGS)

Born in Philadelphia, Pennsylvania, Picardo appeared in TV episodes of *Sabrina, the Teenage Witch* and *The Outer Limits*, before gaining fan notoriety as werewolf Eddy Quist in Joe Dante's *The Howling* and as The Doctor on *Star Trek: Voyager*. California resident, Picardo continues to work in TV episodes of *Masters of Horror*, *Stargate: Atlantis* and *Stargate: SG-1*.

Since Joe Dante stole my fire with "Eddy Quists's Howlin' good, lipsmackin' Ribs," (page 173) I'm enclosing this personal tribute to The Godfather Movies:

INGREDIENTS

STOOL PIGEON	2½ - 3	pounds boneless, skinless chicken breast
BLOODY POOL	4	cups thick tomato sauce (your favorite store brand or see separate recipe)
SEVERED TONGUE	2-3	red bell peppers, cleaned and sliced in triangular pieces
BULLET CASINGS	1-1½	pounds Italian turkey sausage, sweet or hot as desired, cut in chunks (before cooking) with poultry shears
PANTRY ITEMS	Olive Oil	
	Garlic	
	Salt and pepper	
	Flour	

If you want to make your own sauce before stool pigeon preparation, use the following sauce:

SAUCE:

2 tablespoons olive oil

3 cans Italian plum tomatoes, drained and slightly pureed so still chunky

4 cloves garlic, pressed

1 tablespoon fresh basil, fresh

1 teaspoon sugar or more if stoolie had high "blood sugar"

Salt and pepper

¾ teaspoon oregano

1 large carrot

DIRECTIONS

THE SAUCE

Lightly brown pressed garlic in olive oil. Add tomato, sugar and all seasonings and bring to bubble; reduce heat. Add carrot broken into 2-3 large chunks to absorb acidity and simmer 1 hour. Remove carrot chunks before using. Set aside and turn your attention to that lousy stoolie.

THE STOOLIE

Wash and dry chicken breast; cut each breast into 2-3 medallions (cut on diagonal and pound slightly) and roll each piece in flour.

Before cooking chicken, sauté pepper triangles in one tablespoon olive oil over medium heat. Add salt and pepper. After 5-10 minutes and edges of peppers are slightly brown, set aside.

Brown chicken in olive oil on each side with 2-3 cloves of the pressed garlic. You can re-use the pepper sauté pan if you're a cheap, lazy bastard.

At the same time, cook turkey sausage chunks on medium-high heat. If you got half a brain, you'll realize this is what to use the pepper sauté pan for.

Do I have to tell you everything?

When chicken is browned and sausage chunks are cooked through, combine them along with pepper slices in large pan and put two-three cups of tomato sauce over them.

Stir and simmer over low heat until chicken is cooked through.

Serve with side of pasta, using extra tomato sauce, a green vegetable sautéed in garlic and oil, crusty bread, cheap wine and a note that says "Don't let this happen to you.

HORROR: THE FOOD RULES

When attending strange religious ceremonies with lots of chanting, do not eat the food.

When a mysterious object moves towards you slowly, run away. Do not stand there and scream or wait to see how fast it eats you.

If a person groans and walks towards you, leave the area quickly.

If you're possessed, don't eat pea soup.

Never look inside a giant egg that is opening especially if it's in the forest or on an alien planet.

Don't eat gooey stuff bubbling out of the ground.

If a vampire comes to your door, do not ask him if he'd like to come inside for a bite.

Never go to a vampire's house for dinner, unless you want to be dinner.

Any plant bigger than you is a man eating plant and should be avoided at all costs.

Never go into the kitchen alone after sex.

Don't eat any food that cooks on the kitchen counter without any visible heat source.

Do not bring desserts or sugar when picnicking in the dessert, especially if you are near a nuclear blast site. Sugar attracts giant insects.

Don't eat any strange meat that tastes like chicken.

Avoid over-eating rich desserts. You will end up dead.

Never drink alcohol if you are underage. You'll die a violent death within five or six scenes.

The last one to leave the table is the next one to die.

Never eat food from a lavish table setting in an abandoned house, no matter how good it looks.

Be wary of overly kind strangers who want to take you home and feed you to their man eating plants/demons/pet mutated whatever…

When taking home an exotic pet, remember to follow the feeding rules very carefully.

Never be the first one to swallow a pill. Wait until your party has done so and see what happens to them. Ditto for any type of food you don't recognize.

If for any reason your food should suddenly turn into slugs, grubs or any species of insect, close your eyes for three seconds and open them again. Your food will return to normal. It's probably a ghost or poltergeist having fun with you.

When it comes to repelling vampires, you'll find garlic doesn't work any where near as well as you think it does.

Always make sure your food is dead before eating.

Do NOT keep food in your basement.

JOHN LANDIS'S
ROAST CHICKEN WITH ONIONS

Producer-director John Landis, who was born in Chicago, Illinois; started out doing stunts in Europe and made his directorial debut with *Schlock (1973)* and followed with the huge hit Animal House. Landis is best known for his directorial work on *The Blues Brothers, An American Werewolf in London* and the epic Michael Jackson video *Thriller.* Landis, a horror film enthusiast, continues to work in Hollywood.

I am afraid that I am not that much of a cook. I am, however, a serious carnivore, so any meat item such as prime rib, steak, chops, etc. is always welcome.

Before I had to watch my weight, I used to take a chicken, stuff it with whole onions and cloves of garlic, then drape the entire thing with bacon and roast it. I am sure it was serious heart attack food, but always delicious. The onions would be especially soft and tasty.

JOHN AGAR'S
CHICKEN WITH CRANBERRIES

INGREDIENTS

1	can whole cranberries	1	package onion soup mix
1	bottle French dressing	4-6	chicken breasts, skinned and boned

DIRECTIONS

Mix first three ingredients well. Put chicken in greased casserole and spoon sauce over chicken.

Cover and bake 350°F for 1 hour.

JUNE WILKINSON'S
POLYNESIAN CHICKEN

INGREDIENTS

½ cup flour

1 teaspoon ground ginger

1 teaspoon salt

½ teaspoon pepper

1 2½ -3 pound broiler fryer chicken, cut into pieces

2 teaspoon salad oil

1 can (16 ounce) tropical fruit salad

1 cup chicken bouillon

⅓ cup toasted flaked coconut

2 tablespoons soy sauce

DIRECTIONS

Combine flour, ginger salt and pepper. Dredge chicken in flour mixture. Brown in hot oil. Drain. Drain fruit, reserving syrup. Add reserved syrup, bouillon, coconut and soy sauce to chicken. Bring to boil, reduce heat and simmer, covered for 30 minutes. Add fruits. Heat. Serve with steamed rice or rice pilaf, if desired.

Serves: 4

TAG LINES

"IT'S 36 FEET LONG, WEIGHS 2000 POUNDS, LIVES 50 FEET BELOW THE CITY. NOBODY KNOWS IT'S DOWN THERE EXCEPT THE PEOPLE IT EATS."
- ALLIGATOR (1980)

"THEY LOVE EVERY MAN THEY MEET: FIRST TO DEATH, THEN FOR DINNER."
- CANNIBAL GIRLS (1973)

"FIRST THEY GREET YOU, THEN THEY EAT YOU."
- BLOOD DINER (1987)

YVETTE VICKERS'S
CHICKEN STIR-FRY ON A BED OF BROWN RICE

INGREDIENTS

1	chicken, cut up	¼	cup white wine
2	tablespoons olive oil	1	lemon
2	garlic cloves	1	tomato
¼	soy sauce		Broccoli
1	onion, sliced into rings		Zucchini
			Tabasco

DIRECTIONS

In a wok brown chicken pieces (mouth size) in olive oil. When done put aside and pour out fat.

Add to wok olive oil, onion rings, zucchini, broccoli, and garlic. Stir fry until done to taste. Add soy sauce and white wine, a squeeze of lemon and tomato. Now, return the chicken to the wok and season with salt and pepper, a dash of tabasco and toss. Serve with steamed brown rice.

Serves: 2 to 4

WHEN POULTRY ATTACKS!

Poultrygeist: Night of the Chicken Dead (2006) – A fried chicken chain builds a restaurant on an Indian burial ground and zombie chickens rise up in this send up of the fast food industry.

Food of the Gods (1976) – Giant chicken attacks a farmer after eating super chicken feed in this Bert I. Gordon "Big" movie.

The Giant Claw (1957) – A giant buzzard like thing is unstoppable due to it's own force field.

The X from Outer Space (1967) – A giant chicken-lizard rampages Japan after hatching from spores on a UFO.

Beaks: The Movie (1987) – When a farmer gets attacked by his chickens, a reporter investigates in this Italian movie sold as a prequel to *The Birds.*

KAREN BLACK'S
BAKED CINNAMON CHICKEN

This recipe is very easy. There's nothing to it. It is delicious and makes a beautiful scent in the whole house.

INGREDIENTS

1	whole chicken, cut up	2	sweet potatoes
2	chicken thighs or legs	3	cinnamon sticks
1	winter squash, seeded and quartered	½	cup chicken broth
			Green apples
		6-8	prunes

DIRECTIONS

Place the chicken in a 11x17 baking dish and add salt and freshly ground pepper. Add chicken broth to cover the pan about ¾ of an inch. Add the cinnamon sticks and winter squash.

Cook at 375ºF for half an hour. Add the sweet potatoes, prunes and apples and cook an additional half hour.

If you're going to drink a wine with this, just make sure it's Francis Coppola's Diamond merlot.

Serves: 4 to 6

OOPS!

In *The Shining (1980)*, the sandwich that Danny (Danny Lloyd) eats early in the movie changes from a few bites to almost entirely eaten in just a few seconds.

During a lunch scene with Norman in *Psycho (1960)*, Marian (Janet Leigh) splits the same loaf of bread three times.

JOHN BUD CARDOS'S
CHICKEN BREAST DIJON

Cardos has developed his career by trying his hand at almost all aspects of film-making, including stunt work, acting, production management, producing and directing. Some of Cardos's better known films include *The Dark* and *Kingdom of the Spiders*.

INGREDIENTS

4	large chicken breasts		Juice of 1 to 1½ limes
½	teaspoon salt or to taste	3	tablespoons chopped parsley
½	teaspoon black ground pepper	2	teaspoons Dijon mustard
4	tablespoons butter	¼	cup chicken broth
5	tablespoons olive oil	4	tablespoons Cognac
2-3	chopped green onions very fine		

DIRECTIONS

Cut chicken breasts in half length wise to make them thinner. Sprinkle with salt and black pepper.

Heat half the butter and olive oil in large fry pan.

Cook chicken over high heat 2 minutes each side. Transfer to a warm plate or platter.

Add green onions, lime juice and parsley and mustard to the pan. Cook 15 seconds, stirring constantly.

Add broth and stir until sauce is smooth. Add in the rest of the oil, butter and cognac.

Pour sauce over chicken and serve immediately.

"WHAT'S THE MATTER, COLONEL SANDURZ? CHICKEN?"

- DARK HELMET (RICK MORANIS)
SPACEBALLS (1987)

SELECTED GENRE FILMOGRAPHY

JOHN 'BUD' CARDOS

FEATURES:

Second Unit Director:
The Incredible 2-Headed Transplant (1971)

House of Terror (1975)

Director:
Kingdom of the Spiders (1977)

The Dark (1979)

The Day Time Ended (1980)

Night Shadows (1984)

Outlaw of Gor (1989) (Stunts)

Nightmare In Wax (1969)

Horror of the Blood Monsters (1970)

Death Dimension (1978)

Actor:
Nightmare In Wax (1969)

Blood of Dracula's Castle (1969)

GODZILLA VS. THE TERIYAKI CHICKEN

INGREDIENTS

2	boneless chicken breasts	1	tablespoon medium dry sherry
4	tablespoons soy sauce, preferably low sodium	2	teaspoons ginger root
		1	clove garlic minced

DIRECTIONS

Mix soy, sherry, ginger root and garlic. Place the chicken breasts in a glass dish and add the remaining ingredients. If the breasts are thick, butterfly them first to reduce cooking time and keep them moist. Refrigerate for 1-4 hours.

Drain the chicken and discard the marinade. Brush a grill pan with oil and heat. Cook about 4-5 minutes per side. For presentation appeal, halfway through cooking on each side, diagonally turn the chicken so you get a cross pattern on the chicken.

Serves: 2

"WHY DID THE ROBOT CROSS THE ROAD? BECAUSE HE WAS CARBON BONDED TO THE CHICKEN."

- ROBOT (DICK TUFELD)

LOST IN SPACE (1998)

OOPS!

Look closely during the dinner scene in *The Sixth Sense.* A microphone cable is visible through Malcolm's shirt.

From Dusk til Dawn – A character is either eating a hamburger or drinking a beer depending on what the camera angle is used.

DEVILED CHICKEN

INGREDIENTS

8	boneless chicken thighs	2	teaspoons Dijon mustard
	Flour	2	teaspoons Worcestershire sauce
	Salt and pepper		
2	tablespoons of butter	2	teaspoons ketchup
2	tablespoons of vegetable or olive oil	½	cup fresh bread crumbs
1	cup chicken stock	1	teaspoon butter, melted

DIRECTIONS

Put flour, salt and pepper in plastic bag with chicken pieces and shake to coat.

Heat butter and oil in skillet. Brown chicken on both sides and transfer to a casserole dish.

Stir in one tablespoon of the remaining flour in the skillet. Add hot stock and stir well. Mix in mustard, Worcestershire sauce and ketchup. Pour sauce over chicken. Moisten the bread crumbs with 1 teaspoon of melted butter and sprinkle over top of chicken. Add more bread crumbs if necessary. Adding butter to the bread crumbs makes a crisp topping. Bake at 350° for 30-40 minutes.

Serves: 4

FREDDIE FRANCIS:

I remember visiting the home of the late Michael Carrerras of Hammer Films, together with my great friend the Hammer producer and writer Jimmy Sangster. The lunch which was served to us was Deviled Chicken. Somewhat appropriate you might think.

RAY HARRYHAUSEN
ROAST DUCKLING WITH APPLE STUFFING

OUR PICK

Harryhausen, born in Los Angeles, California, is second to none when it comes to modern stop-motion animation. Harryhausen advanced his visual effects work with *Mighty Joe Young* and has created many classics since including *The Beast from 20,000 Fathoms*, *Jason and the Argonauts*, *One Million Years B.C.* and *Clash of the Titans*. In 1992 Harryhausen received his honorary Academy Award Oscar handed to him by his old friend Ray Bradbury. Harryhausen divides his spare time between the UK and Spain.

INGREDIENTS

5-6	pound duckling	1	cup dry white wine
	Salt and pepper		

DIRECTIONS

Rinse the duckling inside and out with cold water and pat it dry. Stuff with apple stuffing (recipe below) and truss the bird. Rub with butter or oil and sprinkle with salt and pepper. Prick the skin with a fork to allow the fat to run off. Place the duckling breast side up on a rack in a roasting pan.

Roast at 400°F for 30 minutes. Remove from the oven and drain off the fat. Reduce the heat to 350°F. Add one cup of white wine and baste often. Cook for another 60 minutes or until the internal temperature reaches 180°.

For a crispy skin, brush the duckling with honey 15 minutes before removing from the oven. Let it rest for 10 minutes before carving.

Serves: 4

APPLE STUFFING

INGREDIENTS

2	medium onions, finely chopped	1	teaspoon chopped parsley
4	tablespoons butter	½	teaspoon thyme
2	cups fresh white bread crumbs		Salt and pepper
		5	Granny Smith apples

DIRECTIONS

Cook onions in butter until soft. Add bread crumbs and herbs and cool the mixture.

Peel, core and quarter the apples. Cook in butter until soft. Add to the bread crumb mixture. Cool before stuffing the duck.

Option: For a simpler version, instead of using the apple stuffing, stuff it with one onion sliced, one apple peeled, cored and quartered and one celery stalk with leaves

---

MOVIE FOOD CREDITS

Class of Nuke 'Em High Part II: Subhumanoid Meltdown (1991)

"Key Gripe: Food Stinks"
"Nothing Special Effects: Food on Troma Movie Set"

Microwave Massacre (1983)

"Remember, dismember a friend for lunch!"

Shadow Creature (1995)

"No Zebra Mussels were harmed during the filming of this production."

"Correction:

After filming, a water bag containing dead Zebra Mussels was found. This movie is dedicated to the few..."

Dead Meat (1993)

"No fish were harmed during the making of this film. But they sure tasted good at the wrap party!"

Killer Tomatoes Strike Back! (1990)

"ASPCT Approved: No friendly tomatoes were injured during the production of this motion picture."

Aliens, Dragons, Monsters and Me (1986) (Himself)

Dinosaur Movies (1993) (Himself)

Mighty Joe Young (1998)

The Sci-Fi Boys (2006) (as Himself)

FAVORITE FOODS:

Meatloaf, Roast Duck, Good Steak

FAVORITE DRINKS:

Fruit Juice, 7 up, Ginger ale

SET FOOD:

Very good food, particularly in Spain

EVELYN ANKERS'S
TUTU'S CHICKEN HAWAIIAN

INGREDIENTS

- ½ cup onion, chopped
- 2 pounds cut up chicken pieces (I use boneless, skinless thighs and breasts)
- ½ cup Haupia Mix or Coconut Snow
- 1 tablespoon grated fresh ginger, or 1 teaspoon powdered

- 1 can cream of mushroom soup
- 1 can cream of chicken soup
- ¾ cup banana (firm), sliced
- ¼ cup dry cooking sherry
- ½ cup chicken broth

DIRECTIONS

Sprinkle the chicken with onion and cook chicken uncovered fat side up if skin on or covered with foil if using boneless/skinless chicken in 9x12 baking dish. Cook until just cooked through, 30 minutes at 325°F.

If you are using boneless, skinless chicken, cover with foil while cooking, about 20 – 25 minutes. If you are using bone in and skin on, bake uncovered about 30 minutes. Then, pour the heated sauce over the chicken and cook uncovered for an additional 30 minutes or until bubbly and the chicken is fork tender.

Baste chicken a few times while cooking if using chicken with skin. Drain juice into measuring cup after removing fat.

To make the sauce: mix together Haupia Mix, ginger, soup and bananas in separate pot. Cook gently till it boils and then add cooking sherry and reserved liquid broth from cooked chicken. Pour the hot sauce over chicken and roast another ½ hour or until tender. Sprinkle with paprika and coconut before serving.

PETER CUSHING'S
ORANGE CHICKEN

Born in Kenley, Surrey, England; Cushing left theatre behind to work in Hollywood in the early 1940's with Laurel and Hardy among others. It was not until his landmark role as Baron Victor Frankenstein that he became a household name. A true gentleman, Cushing continued to delight film fans, most notably with Hammer Films productions. He became known to a whole new generation with his portrayal in *Star Wars* as the nefarious Grand Moff Tarkin.

This recipe was made often for Mr. Cushing by his secretary Joyce Broughton.

INGREDIENTS

4	chicken breasts
2	onions, finely chopped
	Mixed herbs

Fresh orange juice and rind of 2 oranges

DIRECTIONS

Lightly fry chicken on both sides. Put into large baking dish and spread with onion, mixed with herbs. Pour orange juice and sprinkle the rind on top.

Bake with foil over the dish for about 30 minutes in oven at 350°F. Remove foil and bake for a further 30 minutes.

For dessert, serve apple pie and ice cream.

"THANK YOU FOR THE COFFEE. IT WAS UNSANITARY BUT DELICIOUS."
MARY HENRY (CANDACE HILLIGOSS)
CARNIVAL OF SOULS (1962)

SELECTED GENRE FILMOGRAPHY

PETER CUSHING
(1913-1994)

www.petercushing.co.uk

FEATURES:

The Curse of Frankenstein (1956)

The Abominable Snowman (1957)

Horror of Dracula (1958)

The Revenge of Frankenstein (1958)

The Mummy (1959)

The Brides of Dracula (1960)

The Gorgon (1964)

She (1965)

The Skull (1965)

Torture Garden (1967)

Frankenstein Must Be Destroyed (1969)

The Vampire Lovers (1970)

Tales From the Crypt (1972)

Asylum (1972)

The Creeping Flesh (1973)

Madhouse (1974)

The Ghoul (1975)

Star Wars (1977)

Shock Waves (1977)

The Uncanny (1977)

House of the Long Shadows (1983)

Biggles (1986)

RICHARD ANDERSON'S FAVORITE
GIANT CHICKEN POT PIE

Anderson appeared as Chief Engineer Quinn in the classic *Forbidden Planet*. Anderson had a prolific career in television and films but it his role as Oscar Goldman in *The Six Million Dollar Man* series that made him a household name. Anderson still attends film conventions and resides in California.

INGREDIENTS

1	package frozen peas		3	tablespoons flour
1	package of frozen carrots		Salt and pepper	
2	Yukon gold potatoes, cubed and cooked		½	cup chopped onion
1½	cups chicken stock		⅔	cup milk
1	tablespoon olive oil		3	cups cooked chicken, cubed
3	tablespoons unsalted butter		1	package of puff pastry

DIRECTIONS

Pre-heat oven to 425°F.

Heat the stock in a saucepan and allow to simmer.

Add the oil to a pan and sauté the onion until soft.

In a pan heat the butter over low heat and stir in the flour. Stir flour and butter for 3 minutes until the flour is well cooked. Add the heated stock to the pan and stir with a wooden spoon or whisk until smooth. When the mixture starts to boil, reduce heat and continue heating and stirring until the sauce thickens between 5-10 minutes.

Add the chicken and vegetables to the stock mixture and remove from heat.

Pour the filling into a baking dish and top with puff pastry. Pinch edges and flute. Cut a slit on the top to allow steam to escape.

Bake for 25-30 minutes or until golden brown.

Favorite quote: "Don't know much about acting... but don't ever get caught doin' it," — Gary Cooper

FROM THE SEA

JUNE WILKINSON'S
TURBAN MOUSSE

INGREDIENTS

½ cup fumet or clam juice

½ cup water

¼ cup butter

Salt

1 cup sifted flour

2 large eggs plus 2 egg whites

White pepper and nutmeg

⅓ cup heavy (35%) cream

6 snapper, sole or flounder fillets

½ pound sole or flounder fillets ground very fine, 1 cup

DIRECTIONS

Bring liquid to boil and melt butter in it. Add salt and flour all at one time and beat mixture over moderate heat until it forms a ball.

Add eggs, one at a time beating completely after each addition. Add one egg white, beat well, add second egg white. This is a panade. Keep cool over ice.

Place one cup ground fish in a mixing bowl and combine with one cup of panade. Place bowl over ice and add seasonings.

Add cream very slowly beating constantly so mixture remains firm.

Butter a 4-6 cup ring mold very well and line with scored fillets so that ends hang over outside rim.

Pack mousse into mold over fish and turn ends over the mixture. Cover with buttered foil and chill for 1 hour.

Set mold in a pan of water and place in lower third of 375°F oven and bake 45 minutes or until knife inserted comes out clear.

Unmold onto a hot buttered platter.

Serves: 6

RICHARD FLEISCHER'S
MENU ABOARD THE SUBMARINE NAUTILUS

Born in Brooklyn, New York, Richard Fleischer was the son of famed animator Max Fleischer and nephew of Dave Fleischer. Fleischer's Hollywood work as a director includes incredible action, film noir oriented pictures and the Disney fantasy classic *20,000 Leagues Under the Sea*. Fleischer went on to work with many Hollywood greats until his retirement in 1989.

December 8th, 1868

As served by Captain Nemo to his distinguished guests: Professor Aronnax and his assistant, Conseil, and the noteworthy harpoonist, Ned Land.

APPETIZER

Fillet of Sea Snake

ENTREE

Brisket of Blowfish with Sea Squirt Dressing basted in Barnacles

DESSERT

Saute of Unborn Octopus garnished with Sea Cucumber Preserves

N.B.: Milk of Giant Sperm Whale will be served during dinner

Bon Appetit

APRES DINNER

Seaweed cigars will be offered in the lounge

ALFRED HITCHCOCK'S
MOUSSE OF SOLE

INGREDIENTS

½ pound fresh fillet of sole

½ cup cold béchamel sauce (page 100)

4 tablespoons fresh dill

1 egg

1 cup heavy (35%) cream

Salt and pepper

DIRECTIONS

Place the sole in a food processor and process until finely ground up.

Add the egg, salt and pepper and beat for a few minutes. Turn to low speed and slowly pour in the béchamel sauce.

Then add the cream in small amounts at a time until smooth. Test one small spoon in boiling water and correct the seasoning if necessary.

Pour the mixture in a buttered mold. Cover and bake in the oven in a pan of water for about 30 minutes at 350°F.

DEATH BY FOOD

Sleepaway Camp (1983) – An unsavory chef gets his just desserts by being cooked with the corn on the cob.

Se7en (1995) – In their first assignment together, detectives David Mills (Brad Pitt) and Lt. William Somerset (Morgan Freeman) discover a gruesome crime scene in a filthy, cockroach-infested apartment in which an obese man lies dead, face-down in a huge bowl of spaghetti.

Theatre of Blood (1973) – A Shakespearean actor (Vincent Price) takes revenge upon the critics who gave him bad reviews. Robert Morley plays one such victim who is force fed pie made from his beloved pets while another, Robert Coote, is drowned in a barrel of wine.

Raiders of the Lost Ark (1981) – "Bad Dates" An attempt to poison Indiana Jones goes awry but yields one innocent casualty.

The Sixth Sense (1999) – Bad soup.

Hannibal (2001) – Bad brain.

Thinner (1996) – A harmless looking pie holds a gypsy curse.

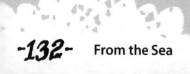

IRVIN KERSHNER'S
LUMMI ISLAND GRAVELOX

Born in Philadelphia, Pennsylvania, Kershner started making documentary films until he was given work by producer Roger Corman in 1958. Kershner, who now teaches film, went on to direct *Eyes of Laura Mars*, *Star Wars: Episode V – The Empire Strikes Back* and the last Sean Connery James Bond film *Never Say Never Again*.

This I call Lummi Island Gravelox. Many of the stars and actors with whom I have worked have enjoyed it. Of course on Lummi Island in the San Juan Islands, I would make it with salmon that I have just caught. However, any fresh salmon will do. In fact even farm raised salmon, which is very fatty, compared to wild salmon, seems to make a presentable dish.

INGREDIENTS

About 1 pound of salmon fillet (pull out the bones with pliers)

Milk

Kosher salt

Sugar

Dill

DIRECTIONS

Marinate the salmon in milk for about 2 hours in the fridge.

Meanwhile...

In a glass or plastic container, mix five parts of the salt and one part sugar, half white and half raw brown sugar.

With scissors, cut up fresh dill very finely and mix with the salt-sugar mixture. Be sure to use plenty of dill!

Rinse the fillet and place in a container. Rub the fish all over with the salt-sugar-dill combination. Sprinkle with a dash of cracked black pepper.

Place fish on an inverted shallow plate that sits in a larger plastic or glass container.

Place another plate on top and put a large can of juice or a clean brick on top of the plates. Cover the set-up with plastic wrap. This set-up allows the fish to drain.

Let sit in fridge for 2 days.

SELECTED GENRE FILMOGRAPHY

IRVIN KERSHNER (1923-)

TV:

Amazing Stories (1986)

SeaQuest DSV (1993)

FEATURES:

Eyes of Laura Mars (1978)

Star Wars: Episode V: The Empire Strikes Back (1980)

Never Say Never Again (1983)

RoboCop 2 (1990)

For variations:

Rub some fresh garlic on the fish before salting. Use only brown sugar.

Slice very thinly. The more surface, the more flavor.

Soak the slices in cold water for a few minutes unless you like a saltier flavor.

Eat on a toasted bagel with a thin slice of onion or use in an omelet — very good!

Covered, and kept in fridge it keeps for at least a week. Remember, slice thinly!

Barbra Streisand loves it. Robert Shaw adored it. Klaus Maria Brandauer was ecstatic. Sean Connery never ate it. Harrison Ford likes it on thin crust pizza.

WHAT'S EATING YOU?

The Seafood

It Came from Beneath the Sea (1955) – A giant octopus tries to eat the Golden Gate bridge in San Francisco.

Attack of the Crab Monsters (1957) – "From the depths of the sea... a tidal wave of terror!" according to the film's tag line. Don't forget the garlic butter.

Piranha (1978) – Deadly Piranha start eating guests a resort in this deadly funny movie from Joe Dante.

Jaws (1975) – A giant shark starts feeding on New England vacationers that both kick started the Hollywood blockbuster and Steven Spielberg's directing career.

Leviathan (1989) – A deep sea diving crew brings up mysterious cargo from a sunken ship that turns them into fish creatures in this watery retread of Alien.

Gamera (1965) – A flying fire breathing turtle savages Tokyo in this Japanese spin off of Godzilla. Yeah, you read that right — a flying, fire breathing turtle.

20000 Leagues Under the Sea (1954) – The Nautilus submarine battles a giant squid in a raging storm in one of the films most memorable scenes.

Voyage to the Bottom of the Sea (1961) – A giant squid attacks an advanced submarine in this scene similar to *20000 Leagues Under the Sea*.

Mysterious Island (1961) – A giant crab attacks escaped civil war prisoners of war who land on a mysterious island in this fine adaptation of the Jules Verne story.

ROD TAYLOR'S
SALMON EN CROUTE

Born in Sydney, New South Wales, Australia, Taylor is best remembered by fans for his starring role in the classic 1960 adaptation of *The Time Machine*. Taylor also appeared in Alfred Hitchcock's *The Birds* and in an early original *Twilight Zone* episode. Taylor continues to work and resides in California.

INGREDIENTS

1	package of puff pastry sheets	1	5 ounce carton garlic herb cheese spread
1	large salmon fillet	1	package chopped spinach
	Salt	1	large egg
	Ground Pepper	2	tablespoons water
			All-purpose flour

DIRECTIONS

Pre-heat oven to 400°F. You might as well put a couple of bottles of Australian Chardonnay on ice too.

On a floured surface roll out a pastry sheet which should be twice the size of your salmon.

Transfer pastry to a cookie sheet.

Place salmon on top, sprinkle with salt and pepper.

With spatula, spread the cheese over top and sides of the salmon.

Having thawed the spinach, spread it on top of the cheese.

Beat the egg and water and brush on the pastry around the salmon.

Fold the pastry over the salmon, like a pastie crimp the edges with a fork. Brush the top of your creation with more beaten egg. Place in the oven and pour yourself a glass of the chardonnay because it will take about 25-30 minutes or until golden brown.

Bon appetit.

SELECTED GENRE FILMOGRAPHY

ROD TAYLOR (1930-)

TV:

Studio 57 (1957)

The Last Day On Earth (1955)

The Twilight Zone (1959)

Tales of the Unexpected (1980)

FEATURES:

World Without End (1956)

The Time Machine (1960)

Colossus and the Amazon Queen (1960)

The Birds (1963)

The Fantasy Film Worlds of George Pal (Himself): (1985)

Time Machine:

The Journey Back (Himself): (1993)

All About 'The Birds' (Himself): (2000)

The Warlord: Battle For the Galaxy (1998)

K.A.W. (2006)

ALFRED HITCHCOCK'S
FILETS OF SOLE BONNE FEMME

INGREDIENTS

4	Dover sole fillets	2	tablespoon butter
6	shallots	3	tablespoon olive oil
½	pound mushrooms	1	cup white wine
2	tablespoon parsley	2	cups heavy cream
	Salt and pepper	2	tablespoon lemon juice

DIRECTIONS

Butter a fish dish. Mince some shallots, mushrooms and parsley and lay them in the dish. Place the fillets on top, add salt, pepper and pieces of butter. Pour white wine over, cover and cook in oven for 15 minutes. Take out the sole and keep it warm on a dish. Reduce heat on the sauce. Add cream and butter, mixing well. Add a few drops of lemon juice at the very end. Finally brown under broiler.

Serves: 4

FISH STORIES

Godzilla (1998)

2,000 foam fish were made to create a huge fish pile to lure Godzilla.

Small Soldiers (1998)

The piranha fish next to Alan's computer is a reference to Piranha (1978), also directed by Joe Dante.

Alien (1979)

For a scene involving the dissection of a dead 'face-hugger' alien, the FX department created realistic looking guts by using actual seafood inside the shell of the alien. There are mussels on the outside and oysters and squid in the middle.

It Came from Beneath the Sea (1955)

Due to budget and time constraints, effects pioneer Ray Harryhausen created the octopus with only six arms. Two arms are always shown in the water so he could get away with the effect.

MARGUERITE CHAPMAN
POACHED SALMON WITH HOLLANDAISE

OUR PICK

Born in Chatham, New York, Chapman co-starred in the early sci-fi Republic serial *Spy Smasher* and played Alita in the 1951 space saga *Flight to Mars*. Chapman's last science fiction film was in Edgar G. Ulmer's *The Amazing Transparent Man*.

INGREDIENTS

6	salmon fillets, about 6 ounces each		4	parsley sprigs
½	cup dry white wine		2	sprigs fresh dill
½	cup chicken stock or water		2	green onions, chopped
1	tablespoon lemon juice			Salt and pepper

DIRECTIONS

In a skillet, make poaching liquid with wine, stock or water, lemon juice, herbs and chopped green onions. Heat until liquid is simmering. Add salmon skin side down and cover. Cook for 3 to 4 minutes depending on thickness of fillets. Serve with hollandaise sauce or herbed mayonnaise.

Serves: 6

BLENDER HOLLANDAISE SAUCE

3	egg yolks		Dash of white pepper or cayenne
1-2	tablespoons lemon juice	¼	teaspoon salt
		½	cup unsalted butter

Place eggs, juice and pepper in a blender. Heat the butter until it bubbles but make sure it does not brown. Turn blender to high and give it a good whirl for a few seconds. Remove the lid and gradually add the melted butter in a slow steady stream. This takes about 30 seconds. Serve on top of fish immediately.

SELECTED GENRE FILMOGRAPHY

MARGUERITE CHAPMAN (1918-1999)

TV:

Science Fiction Theater (1955)

Strange Stories (1956)

FEATURES:

The Body Disappears (1941)

Spy Smasher (1942)

Flight To Mars (1951)

The Amazing Transparent Man (1960)

RICOU BROWNING
BBQ SHRIMP SCAMPI

Shrimp scampi is actually jumbo shrimp in North America.

Born in Pierce, Florida, Ricou Browning was a natural born swimmer, who appeared in all three *Creature from the Black Lagoon* films as the Creature in the underwater scenes. Browning, a stunt man and writer also worked on the James Bond film, *Never Say Never Again* and currently resides in Florida where he still attends film conventions.

INGREDIENTS

1½	pound of shrimp scampi (in shell)	2	tablespoons roasted sesame oil
½	bulb fresh garlic, pureed	½	cup ginger root, pureed
½	cup basil	½	cup olive oil
		3	smoked jalapenos

DIRECTIONS

Combine ingredients in a bowl and marinate for 2 hours.

Strain marinade. Turn BBQ to high. When it reaches high heat, turn down to minimum. Put shrimp on a 6" skewer from tail end to the head. Throw on the barbecue and 2 to 3 minutes later, they're ready to eat.

Serves: 4

OOPS!

In the fight scene in *Spiderman (2002)*, the food that was on Flash's back from the cafeteria disappears.

Interview with the Vampire: The Vampire Chronicles (1994): Just before the scene where Louis (Brad Pitt) burns the mansion down, Lestat (Tom Cruise) knocks down platters of food. While the mansion burns, the platters of food return to the table.

JEFF WOOLNOUGH'S
SALMON IN THE YURT

Canadian born writer-director Woolnough got his start with an early children's television show *Dracula: The Series* before graduating to prominent science fiction dramas such as *Stargate SG-1* and *Earth: Final Conflict*. Woolnough directed six episodes of *The Outer Limits* between 1997 and 2000. Woolnough also wrote and directed an episode of *Dark Angel* and directed television episodes of *Battlestar Galactica*.

This is my favorite salmon recipe.

DIRECTIONS

Sprinkle a fillet of salmon with soy sauce.

Cover fish with a layer of pickled sushi ginger.

Cover ginger with a layer of thinly sliced fresh lemon.

Place the fish on a large piece of tin foil and form a tent. Place this on the BBQ for approximately 15 minutes. Serve with Chinese plum sauce on the side.

ANECDOTE

Luckily we were filming at a hospital when this happened: Our key grip, who shall remain nameless, was first through the lunch line and he happened to be a fan of spicy food. The caterer, who shall also remain nameless, handed him the 'hot sauce' which this day was housed in one of those roach-coach red plastic ketchup containers, and he proceeded to liberally douse his entire meal with the stuff.

He must have put in a heck of a morning's work because our key grip was hungry and tore into the meal like he was going to the chair. Yet before long he cottoned to the fact that his food had a 'funny' taste. One of the lesser grips performed a taste test and thought he detected a 'soapy' essence. Turned out the hot sauce was really window cleaner and our key grip spent the afternoon in emergency having his stomach pumped because he'd already consumed HALF of his meal!

SELECTED GENRE FILMOGRAPHY

JEFF WOOLNOUGH

TV:

Dracula: The Series (1991)

Stargate SG-1 (1997)

Sleepwalkers (1997)

Earth: Final Conflict (1997)

The Outer Limits (1998-2000)

The Man Who Used to Be Me (2000)

The Invisible Man (2001)

Strange Frequency (2001)

Strange Frequency 2 (2001)

Dark Angel (& writer) (2001)

Taken (2001)

Smallville (2002)

Battlestar Galactica (2005-2006)

FEATURES:

Universal Soldier II:Brothers In Arms (1998)

Universal Soldier III Unfinished Business (1998)

Nightworld: Lost Souls (1998)

PAUL NASCHY
...ON THE BEST OF SPAIN

Paul Naschy is the Spanish equivalent to Lon Chaney and Bela Lugosi having played vampires, werewolves, mad doctors among many other monsters throughout his long career. Not only does Naschy star, he also writes, produces and directs many of his films. He has played werewolf Waldemar Daninsky in more than a dozen films.

My favorite cuisine by far is Spanish, followed by French, Italian and surprisingly enough, Japanese. I must confess that during my stay in Japan it took me a long time to get used to eating raw fish, though I ended up loving it.

Coming back to traditional Spanish food, I enjoy the dishes from all of the Spanish regions: Catalonia, Aragón, Andalusia, the Basque country, Castilla la Mancha, Castilla León, Galicia, Asturias, etc. But as for my favorites, I love shellfish and seafood such as lobster, ox crab, shrimps, king prawns, oysters and so on. The very best place for seafood is the region of Galicia. *(North West of Spain)* I'm also keen on mussels. I adore typical Madrid dishes like boiled tripe, and Madrid "hot pot" *(this is a kind of stew with chick peas, potatoes, and red sausage)* and the marvelous tapas which are served in the classic bars of this great old city.

Tapas are hors d'oeuvres ranging from slices of red garlic sausage, little dishes of chicken and rice, chunks of potato omelette, spicy green peppers, tiny grilled sardines, small squares of tuna fish or minced veal pie, chick peas with cumin, diced liver with onions, boiled cockles, prawns in garlic. The list is endless. Tapas are usually served free in bars to accompany a glass of beer or wine. Needless to say, the bars which serve the most and best tapas get the most patrons. However in some parts of Spain the tapas must be paid for.

I'm partial to red meat, cooked rare, and I like fish too. My favorite species are cod, skipjack, swordfish, horse mackerel, salmon and hake. Other favorite foods of mine include squid, cuttlefish and octopus, especially "Galician style," *boiled and seasoned with olive oil*, sea salt and paprika. I consume my fair share of *Parma style* ham, chorizo sausage, and pork luncheon meat.

Turning to Italian cooking, I'm very fond of pasta. I like cheese very much, first and foremost Spanish cheeses which are strong and aromatic, then French and Dutch. As for wine I prefer red wine, especially the bull's blood red of Rioja wines, although I also enjoy Valdepe, which is more mild tasting. I also like Asturian cider and the Galician Ribeiro, a light, fruity white wine to accompany shellfish.

As for fruit, my preferences are for melon, watermelon and strawberries. I don't like champagne or whisky. I should tell you that I don't cook myself, but Elvira, my wife, is an extraordinary cook who can master any style. Being both Spanish and Italian is a big advantage. Incidentally, I love having meat fondues and "carpacho" *which is meat cooked at the table on individual charcoal grills.* As you can see, besides devouring people on nights of the full moon, Waldemar Daninsky is a lover of good food.

Translated from the original Spanish by Mike Hodges. Notes from the translator are in *Italics*.

SHRIMP AND BEER WITH TOMATOES

Ingredients

1 ½	pounds of pacific white shrimp, deveined and peeled	3	tomatoes, chopped
½	cup of onion, chopped	1	tablespoon parsley, minced
1	tablespoon garlic, minced	1	bottle Beer
2	tablespoons olive oil	2	tablespoons tomato paste
	Salt and pepper		

Directions

In a large pot, heat the garlic and onions in the oil over low heat until soft. Add the shrimp, beer and boil for a few minutes until the color of the shrimp changes to orange. Add the tomatoes and the paste and stir until paste is dissolved. Add parsley and salt and pepper to taste.

Pour in bowls and serve.

Serves: 2

GIANT MUTATED KILLER OCTOPUS (GALICIAN STYLE)

This is a popular dish in Spain. Octopus, when cooked properly, should be tender and not chewy.

INGREDIENTS

1½	pound of shrimp scampi (in shell)	2	tablespoons roasted sesame oil
½	bulb fresh garlic, pureed	½	cup ginger root, pureed
½	cup basil	½	cup olive oil
		3	smoked jalapenos

DIRECTIONS

Thaw octopus in refrigerator for 24 hours. With a sharp knife, remove legs and discard the rest of the octopus. Pour water in a pot large enough to hold the octopus and heat to a rolling boil.

Pound the octopus with a hammer or meat tenderizer repeatedly until soft lest it re-animate and lock you in its steely grip. This also acts to tenderize it.

Simmer the octopus in the boiling water for 1 hour. Add potatoes and simmer an additional 20 minutes. Test thickest part of octopus by poking it with a sharp knife. It should be tender and meet no resistance.

Remove the potatoes, transfer to cutting board and slice them thin. Remove octopus, allow to cool then slice into small bite sized chunks. Place potatoes on serving platter and arrange octopus chunks around potatoes. Drizzle the olive oil over octopus and potatoes, and sprinkle with paprika, and sea salt.

"YOU FORGOT THE OCTOPUS."

- STUDIO LOT EDITOR TO ED WOOD (JOHNNY DEPP).

ED WOOD

SAUT eD LANGOUSTINES WITH GINGER MUSTARD

Langoustines are also known as Dublin Bay prawns or lobsterettes.

Ingredients

- 2 pounds of langoustines, shells cracked
- 1 large red onion, chopped
- 3 cloves minced garlic
- 1 tablespoon of ginger root, grated
- 3 tablespoons pommery mustard
- 1 cup white wine
- 3 tablespoons butter

Directions

Heat olive oil in a pan and add langoustines, onion, ginger and garlic. Saute for 10 minutes. Add mustard and wine. Remove from heat and add butter. Stir and serve.

"IF YOU WERE A LOBSTER MAN, WOULD YOU GO INTO A HAUNTED HOUSE SURROUNDED BY HOT SPRINGS?"

- PROFESSOR PLOCOSTOMOS (PATRICK MACNEE)
LOBSTER MAN FROM MARS (1989)

DYE FISH DYE!!

Star Trek VI: The Undiscovered Country (1991)

During a lavish dinner scene between the Enterprise crew and Klingons, exotic seafood colored blue using vegetable dye was used to create an alien table setting.

Director Nicholas Meyer offered 20 dollars to each actor who would eat the food during a take. William Shatner took up the challange and made several hundred dollars by the end of the production.

The Omen (1976)

When the fishbowl falls to the ground, (dead) sardines painted orange were used in place of actual goldfish, which director Richard Donner refused to kill for the sake of making a movie.

GRILLED TUNA WITH CORN RELISH

INGREDIENTS

4 fresh tuna steaks, 4-6 ounces each

RELISH:

1 large Spanish onion, diced

1 large red pepper, diced

1 large yellow pepper, diced

1 cup corn, fresh, canned or frozen

4 tablespoons butter

1 smoked jalapeno pepper, minced

3 cloves garlic, minced

Salt and pepper

½ cup white wine

1 tablespoon cilantro, chopped

DIRECTIONS

Grill the tuna steaks for 5 minutes each side.

TO MAKE THE RELISH

Put butter in a saucepan. Saute the onion with the peppers, garlic and jalapeno until soft. Add the corn and the wine.

Turn up the heat and reduce the liquid by half. Stir in the cilantro.

Put tuna steaks on a platter and top with the relish.

Serves: 4

"IS THERE A DOCTOR IN THE FISH?"

- BERTHOLD (ERIC IDLE) TRAPPED INSIDE A WHALE.

THE ADVENTURES OF BARON MUNCHAUSEN (1988)

OYSTERS WITH SMOKED GRUYERE AND ARUGULA

INGREDIENTS

- 4 dozen oysters, shucked
- 3 bunches arugula, washed and chopped
- 4 shallots, diced
- ½ pound gruyere, grated
- 3 cloves of garlic, minced
- 1 cup Bechamel sauce
- ½ pound smoked gruyere

DIRECTIONS

Sauté the onions, with the garlic until softened and then add the arugula.

Remove from heat and strain. Put arugla in oyster shell, and top each with an oyster.

Heat the sauce in a sauce pan and add the cheese. Stir until it is thoroughly melted.

Place shells on baking pan and top with the sauce. Put in 350°F oven for 10 minutes until tops are golden brown.

ALEX GORDON

Gordon was such a big movie fan in his early days in Great Britain, along with his brother Richard that he became President of the Gene Autry Fan Club there. Gordon went on to produce and distribute a slew of 1950's science fiction films, including one of Bela Lugosi's last pictures. Gordon went on to work for Gene Autry in the 1970's at Autry's Western Heritage Museum.

POCKET OYSTERS

When I handled publicity for Gene Autry's 1954 British tour, Gene and his wife Ina and Gail Davis (TV's Annie Oakley, produced by Gene) were invited to a fancy night club along with London show people. Someone ordered oysters for everyone to start.

I can't eat oysters, so I pretended to eat them but slipped them into the side pockets of my fancy evening suit. When everyone got up to dance, I was left alone with Gail Davis at the table. She asked if I wanted to dance and I said I wasn't good at it but she said let's try it!

SELECTED GENRE FILMOGRAPHY

ALEX GORDON
(1922-2003)

FEATURES:

Writer:
Bride of the Monster (1955)

Executive Producer:
Day the World Ended (1955)

Producer:
The She-Creature (1956)

Voodoo Woman (1957)

The Atomic Submarine (1959)

The Underwater City (1962)

I had forgotten about the oysters and I'll leave it to your imagination as to how I felt with my sticky wet pockets trying to cling to Gail and whirl around the floor!

HERBERT L. STROCK
...ON ASIAN CUISINE

Boston, Massachusetts born Strock cut his directing teeth on the early sci-fi TV show Science Fiction Theater and went on to direct cult 1950's films like *Gog*, *I Was a Teenage Frankenstein* and *Blood of Dracula*. Strock also directed the Boris Karloff hosted TV show *The Veil* and kept busy up until his passing.

In Tibet while directing several video-tape documentaries about Tibetan life, I ate whatever was served that didn't move: yak meat, pickled vegetables and rice. Breakfasts consisted of pickled vegetables, a cream-of-wheat type of cereal with rock granules of sugar, a little yak milk and tea. Eggs were the size of pigeon eggs, and in fact probably were. Bread was non existent. I brought soda crackers, peanut butter and mayonnaise from home. When we entertained, foodstuff was brought in from China, and the meals became fairly sumptuous.

In Phnom Penh we had the finest French meals one could ask for — langoustines, salmon, filet mignon, and the finest desserts. We were there to film starving refugees from Mali, who fled to Niger in search of water.

In China, only the producer, Lisa Lu, and myself were feasted on the best Chinese banquets by our Chinese dignitary hosts. These banquets were the most sumptuous one could ever sit down to.

We would be invited by some State big-wig, and then we would have to reciprocate with a banquet thrown in their honor. It was a contest to see who could come up with the most spectacular meal at the most outstanding banquet facility. Chinese food in China is a far cry from what we get in Chinese restaurants in this country. They had never heard of chop suey or chow mein.

This feasting went on for weeks. Talk about a meal — from bird's nest soup, Peking Duck, roast pork, fried shrimp, a huge barely cooked fish, dumplings, chicken, beef, vegetables, noodles, rice, and on and on — maybe fifteen or twenty delicacies. Included always was that infamous Mao Tai, probably the closest thing to antifreeze one ever tasted and with a mule's kick to boot. This was followed by a red Chinese sweet wine that soon put our hosts into delirium, but I was able to "Gan Bay" (Good luck) them under the table.

On most locations, despite the budget of the film, I insist that the people working with me are fed a wholesome healthy meal in the middle of the day, so they can keep their energy up.

FREDDIE FRANCIS
....*ON LIVING MOLLUSKS*

Born in Islington, London, England, Francis established himself as a writer and accomplished cinematographer before directing many memorable horror films. He won the Academy Award for the cinematography for *Glory* in 1989 and did the cinematography for David Lynch's *The Straight Story*.

Shortly after completing *The Creeping Flesh* with Peter Cushing, I returned to my house one day and found a parcel on my doorstep. On opening it, I found a box of oysters which had been sent to me by Peter, who lived near Whitstable, one of the great oyster producing bays of the British Isles. They were delicious oysters and Peter was amused when I told him I had returned to find this parcel 'breathing' on the doorstep. This was obviously stretching the truth but it was quite amusing to open a parcel from him and find living mollusks inside.

"HEY, THIS IS REAL SMOKED SALMON FROM NOVA SCOTIA, CANADA, $24.95 A POUND! IT ONLY COST ME $14.12 AFTER TAX THOUGH."
- LOUIS (RICK MORANIS) *GHOSTBUSTERS (1984)*

ALFRED HITCHCOCK'S
SEASONED FISH

INGREDIENTS

1 Sole, Halibut, Striped Bass, Salmon or Turbot fillet

4 shallots, chopped

1 cup dry white wine

1 cup heavy cream

5 tablespoons flour

1 cup fish stock

1 tablespoon butter plus 2 teaspoons

2 egg yolks, slightly beaten

DIRECTIONS

Place the fish seasoned with salt and pepper in a saucepan with one tablespoon of butter and the chopped shallots. Add one cup of dry white wine. Let boil and cook slowly for 12 minutes for filet of sole, 15 to 20 minutes for striped bass, salmon and Turbot.

Meanwhile, in a clean pan, combine four tablespoons of the flour with the two teaspoons of butter and stir until it becomes golden brown. Slowly pour in the fish stock while stirring constantly.

Remove the fish. Cook the liquids until reduced to a third of its original quantity. Add the fish stock sauce and stir to combine with the liquids. Let boil for 5 minutes then stir in the heavy cream.

At the last minute, add the yolks in the sauce but do not boil. Pour the sauce over the fish and serve hot, or glaze under a hot broiler.

Serves: 4

"DEAREST, YOU DIDN'T USE CANNED SALMON, DID YOU?"

- GEOFFREY (GRAHAM CHAPMAN) ABOUT THE MEAL THAT KILLED THE ENTIRE DINNER PARTY GUESTS.

THE MEANING OF LIFE (1983)

MEATS

BELA LUGOSI'S
STUFFED CABBAGE ROLLS

Hungarian born, Lugosi already a star in his native country worked through silent films in the USA as a character actor before becoming synonymous with Count Dracula on both stage and screen. Lugosi starred in some memorable chillers including *White Zombie*, *The Black Cat (1934)* and *The Son of Frankenstein* as Ygor before working on many low budget horror films at Monogram. Lugosi also played a vampire in *The Return of the Vampire (1944)*.

INGREDIENTS

1½   pounds pork shoulder, very lean ground together with

½   pound smoked ham

1   medium onion, chopped and sautéed

2   garlic cloves, pressed

⅓   cup raw rice, cooked

2   whole eggs

1½   teaspoon salt

½   teaspoon paprika

½   teaspoon black pepper

½   teaspoon MSG

2   medium-sized cabbages

2   large cans sauerkraut

1   medium-sized can solid pack tomatoes

Roux (made with 2 tablespoons fat and 2 tablespoons flour and fried until golden brown)

1   ham hock

DIRECTIONS

Mix meat, fried onion, garlic, eggs and rice. Rice should be about one third in bulk as much as meat. Add salt, pepper, paprika and MSG. Core and boil cabbage until leaves are pliable. Remove from water and gently separate; pare down thick part of leaf. Place about ¼ cup of the meat mixture on cabbage leaf, roll up and tuck in at each end. Mix the sauerkraut which has been drained of juice and can of tomatoes; mix in roux. Place a small ham hock in bottom of pan; then a layer of sauerkraut, using about half of it; then place all cabbage rolls on kraut.

Cover with balance of kraut. Cover with enough water to cover contents in kettle. Bring to a boil, reduce heat, cover and simmer for 2½ hours. Serve with a dollop of sour cream on top of cabbage roll. Parsley and buttered potatoes are good to serve with this dish.

RICHARD GORDON
...ON BELA LUGOSI

When I grew up in the Thirties, I had a short spell of anemia. The family doctor prescribed a diet that featured raw liver. To try and make it more palatable, my mother put it on white bread as a sandwich but the result was that the bread became soaked in blood and turned red, running down my chin when I bit into it. Some friends have kindly suggested that this started my love for horror pictures and the great affection I developed for Bela Lugosi and Boris Karloff.

Bela's favorite food actually was stuffed cabbage with generous helpings of sour cream, a Hungarian specialty that his wife Lillian often made at home where my brother and I enjoyed it in their company when they were living in New York. Boris Karloff preferred grilled kidneys when we were lunching in London. Zachary Scott had a particular fondness for prosciutto but it had to be served with figs in place of melon – not always easy to come by, even when specially ordered in advance.

There was always an end-of-picture party on every film, and at the conclusion of *Horror Hospital*, someone suggested that each participant bring a favorite dish from home. Robin Askwith arrived with a girl friend and a batch of delicious cookies for dessert. What he didn't tell us was that they were baked with hash which we only realized after they had been demolished. I had a business acquaintance from America who came to the party and whom I had invited later for a formal dinner at one of London's most exclusive restaurants. He passed out during the hors d'oeuvres and slept through the rest of the meal.

My favorite food and drink: caviar and champagne, of course. What else would you expect from someone who was lucky enough to have worked with Boris Karloff, Bela Lugosi, Peter Cushing and so many other wonderful people before and behind the cameras. It was a wonderful world.

"I AM A MEAT POPSICLE."

- CORBIN DALLAS (BRUCE WILLIS)

THE FIFTH ELEMENT (1997)

BILLY VAN'S
BILLY BEEF

Toronto born Van is best known as The Count, who hosted *The Hilarious House of Frightenstein* children's television show. Van considered "The Librarian" his favorite character on Frightenstein. Van worked primarily in television shows such as *Bizarre* and did voice-over work before his untimely passing.

INGREDIENTS AND DIRECTIONS

Pre-heat oven to 350°F.

Depending on how hungry you are and how soon you want to eat!

In a casserole dish, place:

3	or 4 cups left over beef, cut in decent-sized chunks	2	carrots, cut in round slices
1	or 2 cans whole mushrooms	½	small onion
½	or whole green pepper, diced	1	packet of gravy mix

Add: Oregano, black pepper, garlic powder, HP sauce (a few dashes), to taste.

Add:

1	can mushroom soup, undiluted. Just dabble on top of the mixture, don't mix	1-1 ½	cups water

Cover and cook for about 1½ hours. Give it a stir every now and then. During the last half hour, add a little bistro gravy mix and throw the lid on again.

Serve with rice or mashed potatoes and your favorite vegetable. Something green looks good with it such as broccoli, spinach, green beans or whatever you like.

I haven't tried this yet but I think half a cup or 1 cup of white wine in the mixture would go really well. The rest of the bottle of wine, you can take care of yourself during the cooking of the meal. If there's any wine left over, and you're still on your feet, you can serve it with dinner!

Any leftovers are great to freeze for some later time when the thought of cooking really boggles your mind.

This dish originated from Sunday roast beef dinner. There is usually a good portion of meat left over and this is a nifty way to use the leftovers.

BOOTH COLMAN'S
HUSSAR POT ROAST

Born in Portland, Oregon, Colman worked in early live television, appearing in shows like *Science Fiction Theater*, as well as many movie appearances. Colman played Dr. Zaius in *The Planet of the Apes* television series. Colman also played Ebenezer Scrooge hundreds of times on the stage and can still be seen on television shows such as *Star Trek* and in countless feature films.

INGREDIENTS

- 3 pounds rump or eye of round, cut in a short, thick piece
- 2 cups of your favorite marinade or 2 jiggers of vodka
- 2-3 tablespoons butter
- 2 medium onions, sliced
- Salt and pepper

DIRECTIONS

Blanch meat with boiling marinade; for a blander taste, substitute vodka and sprinkle meat, having first browned it on all sides with hot butter. Transfer to casserole and simmer, tightly covered, together with onions and butter in which meat has browned. Sprinkle occasionally with cold water. When meat is nearly tender (about 1½ to 2 hours) make the following stuffing:

- 2 medium onions, blanched and grated
- 2 teaspoons bread crumbs
- 2 teaspoons butter
- Salt and pepper
- 1 tablespoon flour
- ½ cup soup stock

Mix onions, bread crumbs and butter thoroughly. Slice meat thin, making every incision only part way through the roast. Fill these pockets with stuffing and reassemble into original shape. Return to casserole. Add flour, dusted on top of meat, and soup stock. Allow to simmer another 30 minutes

Serves: 6 to 7

BOOTH COLMAN (1923-)

TV:

Science Fiction Theater (1955)

The Veil (1958)

Thriller (1960)

The Outer Limits (1963)

Voyage To the Bottom of the Sea (1964)

The Wild, Wild West (1965)

I Dream of Jeannie (1965)

The Invaders (1967)

Tarzan (1966)

The Flying Nun (1967)

Planet of the Apes (1974)

Star Trek: Voyager (1995)

FEATURES:

Them! (1954)

World Without End (1955)

Time Travelers (1976)

FAVORITE FOODS:

Just about any seafood, especially Oregon Coast razor clams and crabs, Columbia River salmon.

FAVORITE DRINKS:

A very dry martini before dinner.

ANECDOTE

I used to have dinner about once a week at the home of Stan Laurel and his wife Eda who was Russian. A favorite dish was "Hussar Pot Roast," a Polish dish known as "Pieczen." I liked every bite but Stan preferred his familiar English or Scottish fare, nothing topping a dish of tripe. The half-serious arguments as to the relative merits of British and Russian cookery were right out of a Laurel and Hardy script.

EATING OUT!

Pirates of the Caribbean – An enormous turkey dinner and a green apple await Elizabeth Swann (Keira Knightley) aboard the Black Pearl.

Monty Python and the Meaning of Life (1983) – Maitre d' (John Cleese): "Today, we have for appetizers — excuse me — uh, moules marinières, pâte de foie gras, beluga caviar, eggs Benedictine, tarte de poireaux - that's leek tart - frogs legs amandine or oeufs de caille Richard Shepherd — C'est à dire, little quails' eggs on a bed of pureed mushrooms. It's very delicate, very succulent."

Brazil (1985) – French restaurant sometime in the future. Four separate meals that resemble colored scoops of mashed potatoes: Numero 8: Braised veal in wine sauce (3 green lumps); Numero 2 Duck a l'orange; Numero 1 Crevettes a la mayonnaise et Numero 3: Steak

Eternal Sunshine of the Spotless Mind (2004) – Dinner at Kang's Chinese food for Jim Carrey and Kate Winslet. Chicken.

Love at First Bite (1979) – Count Dracula and Van Helsing face off during a dinner date each trying to hypnotize the other. It fails but enter one easily hypnotizable waiter.

Bram Stoker's Dracula (1992) – A giant Roast Beef dinner with potatoes and peas is enjoyed by Anthony Hopkins and the rest of the gang.

The Fly (1986) – Geena Davis and Jeff Goldblum discuss science experimentation over cheeseburgers.

The Matrix (1999) A traitor philosophically contemplates a giant steak garnished with parsley and sliced carrots.

Men in Black (1997) - Leshko's diner. Two aliens have an important last meeting over pirogi and bugs.

Time After Time (1979) – H.G. Wells discovers McDonalds.

Monsters Inc. (2001) – The Restaurant is named Harryhausen's after animation pioneer Ray Harryhausen.

The Terminator (1984) – Not a fun job for Sarah Connor. Another fun day at work as a child hides his mashed potatoes in her uniform pocket.

Spiderman 2 (2004) – A nice lunch, charming café atmosphere is interrupted by a car crashing through window. Enter the badguy.

CARL GOTTLIEB'S
COMFORTABLY PIQUANT MEATLOAF DINNER

New York City born Gottlieb, an actor and writing working on such network shows as *The Bob Newhart Show*, *All in the Family*, and *The Odd Couple*. He broke out into the world of features for co-writing the screenplay for *Jaws*. Gottlieb also wrote and directed *Caveman (1981)* with Ringo Starr. Gottlieb, also a film producer, keeps busy as an actor these days. He is author of *The Jaws Log*, about the making of the movie *Jaws*.

This meal was designed for close friends who wanted to escape the "dining out" experience; people who I knew would enjoy a tasty home-cooked meal reminiscent of Mom, good cafeterias, old-style roadside diners, and an age before national franchises corrupted the concept of "family dining."

THE MENU:

Green Salad

Meatloaf with Potatoes and Fresh-Cooked Vegetables

Coffee and Dessert

It is not health food, but it is low in saturated fats if alternate suggestions are followed.

Recovering alcoholics may substitute sparkling mineral water and iced tea or lemonade as accompanying beverages.

THE MEATLOAF:

In a large mixing bowl, blend by hand the following:

1 pound ground round or low-fat beef (use sirloin, etc. 7-10% fat, no more)

1 pound ground turkey dark meat

1 pound Italian-style turkey sausage

For those who aren't counting calories or fat grams, blend equal quantities of ground sirloin, ground lamb, and pork sausage.

SELECTED GENRE FILMOGRAPHY

CARL GOTTLIEB
(1938-)

FEATURES:

Director:
Caveman (1981)

Amazon Women on the Moon (1987)

Writer:
Jaws (1975)

Jaws II (1977)

Jaws 3-D (1983)

Actor:
Something Evil (1972)

Jaws (1975)

Season to taste with a well-rounded teaspoon of each of the following:

Sea salt or regular table salt		1¼	cups oatmeal
Black pepper, finely-ground		1	8-ounce can tomato paste or ⅔ cup of a prepared tomato-based spaghetti/marinara sauce
Oregano			
Dill			
Sage		1	egg
Thyme			
(for these last four herbs, you can substitute 2 tablespoons of "herbs de Provence" or similar blend)			

In a separate sauté pan or frying pan, briefly blanch the following in a minimal amount of butter or oil at a high heat, just long enough to soften. Do not overcook. These will become completely cooked when the loaf is in the oven.

1 large onion, chopped small (pieces no larger than ¼")

2 small cloves of garlic, chopped fine.

2 bell peppers (green and red is a nice color combination), also chopped small.

Blend the onions, peppers and garlic into the meat mixture.

Grease a loaf pan or use a non-stick pan.

Press the heavy, well-blended meat mixture into a large loaf pan, or use a couple of smaller pans.

Garnish the top with paprika.

Bake in a moderate oven 350°F for 90 minutes to 2 hours. Use a meat thermometer to judge when it's done at least 165° in the center of the loaf. Some fat will cook out, and the loaf may shrink somewhat, leaving about 1/8" all around in the loaf pan. Let cool for 10 minutes, remove from loaf pan, serve with a brown gravy or any tomato sauce.

Serves: 6 easily, can be stretched to 8

ACCOMPANYING DISHES

STRING BEANS OR ITALIAN VEGETABLES

Quickly steam the beans or other vegetables until a little softer than "al dente," while at the same time melting a half a stick of butter (¼ cup) in a sauce pan. When the butter is completely melted, add ½ cup seasoned bread crumbs and equal amount of finely chopped or slivered almonds. Spoon over freshly cooked veggies on a serving platter.

For the health-conscious, substitute a smaller amount of virgin olive or canola oil, and use finely ground Special K or other low-calorie, no-fat breakfast flakes, and very few nuts.

MASHED POTATOES

Buy good potatoes, peel 'em, cook 'em, smash 'em with butter and little heavy cream, add salt to taste. To be healthy, serve boiled new red potatoes in their skins without butter.

GREEN SALAD WITH A LIGHT VINAIGRETTE DRESSING

Eschew iceberg lettuce, instead use a mix of romaine and butter lettuce and arugala, with modest amounts of cucumber pieces and finely sliced radish or cabbage, to taste.

Serve a robust red wine, such as a Chianti or Burgundy.

Conclude with a strong coffee, and a dessert of your choosing. Tasty cookies and mints are always appreciated at this point in the meal, as is a good Port wine or brandy of a reputable age. Fruit and cheese also sit well with this meal, as does a lengthy post-prandial conversation. Have an extra pot of coffee and plenty of brandy or Port and some cigars, and make a night of it.

Good friends become better, better friends become best friends, and strangers become friends when served this dinner.

CARLA LAEMMLE'S
PORK IN SHRIMP SAUCE
(HOM HA JIN GEE YUK)

Niece of Universal Pictures founder, Carl Laemmle, Carla was a ballerina in the classic 1925 silent Lon Chaney film, *The Phantom of the Opera* and appeared with Dwight Frye in the 1931 version of *Dracula*. Laemmle continues to appear in documentaries and resides in California.

This recipe comes to her from her dear friend, writer-director, Ray Cannon.

INGREDIENTS

1½ to 2 pounds fresh pork, cubed	1-2 tablespoons water
1-2 tablespoons soy sauce	Flour
1-2 tablespoons brandy or rum	2 tablespoons shrimp sauce
	Ginger root, sliced

DIRECTIONS

Combine the soy sauce with equal amount of the brandy or rum, and water. Mix with the pork in a heat-proof bowl. Fry out the pork fat and pour over mixture. Sprinkle with flour and mix together. Spread pork evenly in bowl, then spread a thin coating of the shrimp sauce over it. This may be called "paste," found in Chinese markets. Cover with thinly sliced fresh ginger root about an inch and a half apart over entire surface. Steam uncovered for 40 minutes. Serve with steamed rice. Mmmmm.

"I BROUGHT A PORK CHOP FOR LUCK. MAYBE YOU COULD HANG IT AROUND YOUR NECK."
- SHERRIF HANK KEOUGH (BRENDAN GLEESON)
LAKE PLACID (1999)

CLAUDIA CHRISTIAN'S
MARINADED LAMB CHOPS

A Glendale, California native, Christian writes, performs music, acts, directs and is fluent in many languages. Christian is known by science fiction fans as Susan Ivanova on the popular TV series *Babylon 5*. A British sci-fi show, *Starhyke* is Christian's latest foray into acting and directing. She was voted "sexiest woman in sci-fi" by SFX magazine in 1998.

INGREDIENTS

Lamb chops

Soy sauce

Garlic, crushed

Honey

Pepper

Rosemary, fresh chopped

DIRECTIONS

Combine ingredients in a bowl and marinate chops in the fridge until ready to cook. Longer is better.

Remove chops from marinade and grill on the barbecue on high heat for three minutes a side, turning once.

ANECDOTE

I used to eat pigs knuckles with my grandmother. That's pretty gross.

When I was a kid, my mother who is German used to pack my lunches. God bless her! She would make me things like liverwurst and blood and tongue sandwiches. I was not flooded with lunch dates nor did I ever have the experience of "trading lunches" with other kids.

Sad isn't it?

> "I JUST CAN'T HELP IT, I HAVE THIS UNCONTROLLABLE URGE TO EAT MEAT. RED! RAW! MEAT!"
> - RADEK
> *DAY THE WORLD ENDED, THE (1955)*

SELECTED GENRE FILMOGRAPHY

CLAUDIA CHRISTIAN (1965-)

www.claudiachristian.net

TV:

Quantum Leap (1989)

Space Rangers (1993)

Babylon 5: In the Beginning (1998)

Highlander (1998)

Babylon 5: Thirdspace (1998)

Babylon 5 (1994-1998)

Relic Hunter (2001)

Starhyke (2006)

FEATURES:

The Hidden (1987)

Maniac Cop 2 (1990)

A Gnome Named Gnorm (1990)

Hexed (1993)

The Haunting of Hell House (1999)

Never Die Twice (2001)

Atlantis: The Lost Empire (voice) (2001)

The Garden (2005)

FAVORITE FOODS:

Sushi and Sashimi, A Great Steak, Salads

FAVORITE DRINKS:

Red Wine, Water, Good Champagne

DICK MILLER'S
MILLER SLOP

Miller was discovered by Roger Corman and went on to appear in many of his cult horror film hits. He went on to more memorable performances in *The Terminator*, *Gremlins* and *Star Trek*. Miller continues to work in Hollywood, and is instantly recognizable for his many wild and often offbeat roles.

I'm not a chef, but I am a good short order cook. If it can be made in 15 minutes, I'll try it. My favorite recipe is called "Miller Slop." It's very simple.

INGREDIENTS

1 or 2 pounds of ground beef	1 red pepper
	Handful of mushrooms
1 large onion	1 8-ounce can of tomato sauce
1 celery stalk	
1 green pepper	Garlic powder

Cook meat and drain off the fat. Saute chopped onion, Add chopped celery and peppers and tomato sauce. Add spice to taste (must add garlic powder!) Simmer whole mess 10 minutes. You can pour it over toast or rice or eat it as is. It's messy and delicious.

DRINKS: When I'm in New York, I love egg-creams which means I have an egg cream every 10 or 15 years.

SET FOOD: Anything not nailed down. I'm a real "craft-services" hound. I snack all day long. On an extended run picture, I can gain 10 pounds.

"WE HAVE ENJOYED PREPARING MANY OF YOUR ESOTERIC DISHES. YOUR MONTE CRISTO SANDWICH IS A CURRENT FAVORITE AMONG THE ADVENTUROUS."

- MATHESAR (ENRICO COLANTONI)
GALAXY QUEST (1999)

JOHN BADHAM'S
DRACULA'S BLOODY CHILI

English born, American raised Badham is the son of actress Mary Hewitt and an American army general. After graduating from Yale, he got his start producing and directing for television. Badham then directed the hit *Saturday Night Fever*. His diverse films range from the dramatic *Whose Life Is It Anyway?* to the popular thriller *War Games*.

A combination of great chili cooked with curry make a combination that will jangle the most jaded palate into eternal gratitude.

When Dracula escaped from Professor Van Helsing's stake in Yorkshire, he vowed revenge on all of England. This he did by cursing them with the cooking that has been served in London restaurants for over two hundred years!

He escaped by sea to the Caribbean islands, taking with him secret chili recipes that had been created in the black forests of Romania and Transylvania. The werewolves and vampires tiring of the boring blood that flowed from the people in the countryside, added a clever mixture of Indian and West Indian spices. Even vampires like a variety now and then. "Gosh honey, plain blood again? I sucked that for lunch today!"

The resulting brain blower was kept a deep dark secret by vampires in the islands and Area 51.

Only recently in the well documented X-file investigations of Scully and Mulder, was this secret recipe finally unleashed upon the world. If this recipe is left untrammeled it will set loose a plague of heartburn more devastating than the "I Love You" virus.

CONTINUED...

"YOU EAT ONE LOUSY FOOT AND THEY CALL YOU A CANNIBAL. WHAT A WORLD!"
DAN TORRENCE (JOSEPH BOLOGNA)
BIG BUS, THE (1976)

SELECTED SELECTED GENRE FILMOGRAPHY

JOHN BADHAM
(1939-)

www.badhamcompany.com

TV:

Night Gallery (Associate Producer): (1970)

The Sixth Sense (1972)

FEATURES:

Isn't It Shocking (Director): (1973)

From Time To Time (Disneyland short) (as Executive Producer): (1992)

Director:
Dracula (1979)

Blue Thunder (1983)

WarGames (1983)

Short Circuit (1986)

The Revamping of Dracula (Himself) (Documentary short) (2004)

Ingredients

- 2 pounds chuck steak, cut into thick ½" chunks. (don't use better quality steak or you'll wind up with mush and hate it)
- 3 tablespoons fresh chili powder OR 1

  "Carroll Shelby's chili mix" on sale in most supermarkets in small brown paper bag. (great cheater's shortcut)
- 3 tablespoons hot curry powder, (Yes I know there are many different kinds of curry powders, but for the purposes of this recipe you can use one of the commercial brands. Just make sure its a fresh can. If you can mix your own spices so much the better.)
- 1 tablespoon ginger powder
- 2 teaspoons allspice

Salt, pepper and Accent Seasoning

- 2 cans pinto beans
- 1 can garbanzo beans
- 2 brown onions, chopped
- 1 red bell pepper, chopped
- 1 green bell pepper
- 1 yellow bell pepper
- 1 large can tomato sauce
- 1 large can chopped tomatoes
- 1 cup good imported beer like Heineken. (If you're going to use any brand name American beers, don't bother, you'll just ruin the whole thing!)

Directions

Brown the beef lightly in a skillet, then put into a large pot with the tomato sauce, beer, chopped tomatoes and spices. Let simmer while you do the following:

Brown onions and sauté peppers. Add all this and the beans to your large chili pot.

That's it!

Though everything is basically done, the chili should simmer for thirty minutes or so and — this is critical — let it sit and cool off for at least 2 hours! overnight is even better!! This allows the flavors to blend and permeate the chili.

If you eat it right away, you are missing a real treat.

Serve with chutney, papadum and chopped onions on the side.

If you don't have at least three virgins offer you their necks to bite afterwards, you did something wrong!

"ALL THEY HAVE TO DO IS TO EAT THREE OR FOUR CHILDREN AND THERE'D BE THE MOST APPALLING PUBLICITY."

- DR. CATHETER ON GREMLINS IN THE STATION.

GREMLINS 2: THE NEW BATCH (1990)

RICHARD EDLUND'S
WRATH OF GOD CHILI

Edlund (right) with Harrison Ford Well regarded as a pioneer in the field of visual effects, Edlund first became interested in film through a stint in the Navy. After leaving the service he went to study film at the University of Southern California. He met George Lucas and got the chance to produce effects for his landmark science fiction blockbuster *Star Wars* while working at ILM. He has since won 4 Academy Awards and has been nominated for six others.

Inspired by a recipe recovered from the Lost Ark of the Covenant.

Begin this noble ritual at about 9 to 10 p.m., making sure all ingredients are at hand.

4	pounds of sirloin tips or 4 huge yellow onions	3	pounds, extra-lean ground sirloin
3	Olive oil		Cloves of garlic

First, using He-man's sword, cube the sirloin tips into chunks about the size of the Star of India.

Then cleave the ground sirloin in a similar manner.

With a hungry keen-edged Japanese sushi knife, slice up the yellow onions about 3/16" thick and then quarter the stacks.

Wipe off the knife, and keeping safe distance from its edge, slice many cloves of garlic into slices .005-.010 inches thick.

Heat a large, iron Dutch oven. Add a little olive oil and brown the meat, throwing in some salt. When it's almost done, toss in and partially brown the onions and sprinkle in the garlic; then drain off the grease and put the meat aside in a bowl. Wipe clean the Dutch oven.

This phase is of the greatest, even of Biblical importance:

Making sure that the Dutch oven is heated to a sufficient temperature to bring out the fire of the chili powder and the subtlety of the spices — but not too hot, put in some olive oil and while stirring so as to avoid clumping, cook up a thin paste comprised of the following:

2	4-ounce packages of California chili	Some coriander,
1	4-ounce package of New Mexico chili,	Some black pepper
1	4-ounce package of cumin powder	Some white pepper
	Some fenugreek	Other interesting spices you may find in the cabinet
		A liberal amount of cayenne

I do not specify amounts of some of the spices, but keeping in mind that this is a potent and pungent dish, not a bashful one, a generous amount of these spices (with some restraint in the use of white pepper and cayenne) is called for.

2	bottles Bohemia Beer	2	cans kidney beans
	Oregano	1	can pinto beans
	Honey		Dark rum

Simmer this concoction for 20 minutes or so, then add back the meat, garlic and onions, dousing the mixture with at least one bottle of Bohemia beer. You can now stir in a handful of oregano and a few healthy dollops of honey. Standing guard with another bottle of beer lest the mixture become too dry, cover the Dutch oven and let it simmer for about a half hour.

Now add two large cans of kidney beans, and one large can of pinto beans, more beer as needed and mix it all up with a mighty wooden spoon, being careful not to break the beans. It should be a little thin now, with enough liquid to cook down some. At this point a few shots of good dark rum will serve to alert the angels. I prefer St. James Martinique rum. Replace the cover, see that it's simmering nicely on a low flame and slide *Raiders* or *Poltergeist* into your VCR.

Pour yourself a rum and coke, and make sure to come back to stir the pot during the very few boring spots in either of those movies, or better yet, hit pause. At about two o'clock, stumble back into the kitchen and turn off the stove. The next morning check the consistency of the now matured and most marvelous chili, and add a little water if it's too thick – or add a very little cornstarch if it's too thin. In evaluating chili, its taste, consistency, color and texture are all important aspects.

This will produce enough to feed the multitudes, and if you religiously followed the recipe, be sure to get there early with your bowl because you will be surprised at how quickly the pot will empty!

This Wrath of God chili has been refined and tested at many annual chili cook-offs at ILM and later at Boss Film. The pot that was empty first won!

GUNNAR HANSEN'S
TEXAS CHAINSAW CHILI

Born in Reykjavik, Iceland, Hansen is best known as the demented Leatherface from the original *Texas Chainsaw Massacre* film. Hansen continues to act, write, create film documentaries and still has time for occasional horror, genre film conventions.

The only beans in this chili is human beans.

INGREDIENTS

1	pound ground dead meat	1	tablespoon cumin
1	large can tomatoes, chopped	2	garlic cloves (or more if you wish)
1	regular can chicken stock	1	teaspoon oregano
2	whole chili-pepper pods (Ancho or others) if you have them	1½	teaspoon cayenne pepper
1	medium onion, minced	2	tablespoons masa flour (available at health food stores if you're not already in Texas)
7	tablespoons chili powder		

DIRECTIONS

In a stewpot, brown the "meat" and onions. Add canned tomatoes and chicken stock. Add chili pods. Add garlic, chili powder, cumin, oregano, cayenne.

You can add more cayenne later to make it hotter if you wish.

Cover and simmer for at least an hour, till the liquid is reduced. Remove and discard the whole chili pods.

Mix masa flower with half cup of water and pour in. Allow the chili to come to low boil and thicken.

Tiz ready.

If you wish, top with chopped raw onion and grated cheddar when you serve it. This isn't very TexMex, but it's a tasty addition.

Serves: 4. Serves one "Leatherface."

SELECTED GENRE FILMOGRAPHY

GUNNAR HANSEN

FEATURES:

The Texaas Chainsaw Massacre (1974)

The Demon Lover (1977)

Hollywood Chainsaw Hookers (1988)

Campfire Tales (1991)

Rachel's Attic (2002)

Next Victim (2003)

Chainsaw Sally (2004)

Apocalypse and the Beauty Queen (2005)

Wolfsbayne (2005)

Swarm of the Snakehead (2006)

The Deepening (2006)

Gimme Skelter (2007)

The Forest (2007)

If you must serve beans with your chili, serve it on the side. Here's a good recipe:

PINTO BEANS

Soak a pound of pintos overnight.

Add a can of beer, two crushed garlic cloves, two small chopped tomatoes. Simmer till the beans are cooked and the liquid is thick.

Add half cup of minced cilantro 10 minutes before you take the beans off the heat.

If you want the beans properly spicy, chop up as many jalapenos as you can stand (two or three for beginners) and add them at the start of cooking.

I repeat, serve on the side. Beans should never touch chili.

> "I SUPPOSE YOU'RE WONDERING WHY YOUR SOAKING IN REG'S ELEVEN SECRET HERBS AND SPICES. TOMORROW WE'RE HAVING YOU FOR LUNCH!"
>
> - LORD CRUMB
> *BAD TASTE (1987)*

BEST MEAT MOVIES

Ravenous (1999)

A little seen Mexican-American War/comedy/western/horror film stars Guy Pearce as a recently promoted Captain who gets transferred to an outpost. Things take a turn for the worse when they're visited by a ravenous army Colonel cannibal.

The Texas Chainsaw Massacre (1974)

A family of cannibalistic psychos have a few college students for dinner in this classic that re-invented the horror genre.

Eating Raoul (1982)

The Blands (Paul Bartel, Mary Woronov) are a boring, everyday Los Angeles couple who come up with a bizarre and delightfully murderous way to open a new restaurant.

Spider Baby, or The Maddest Story Ever Told (1968)

A family chauffeur (Lon Chaney Jr.) looks after an inbred family suffering from debilitating illness. When lawyers come to collect on their dilapidated mansion the children get hungry.

Parents (1989)

Young Michael Laemie (Bryan Madorsky) suspects his parents aren't cooking up the usual dinner fare when he begins to wonder where all the meat comes from.

Delicatessen (1991)

In a post-apocalyptic society, food is so rare that it is actually used as currency. The residents of an apartment building above a butcher shop receive the occasional order of meat.

Bad Taste (1987)

Directed by Peter Jackson. Aliens farm humans as the main ingredient for their intergalactic fast food chain "Crumb's Crunchy Delights."

JARREL 'FATHER GEEK' JAY KNOWLES'S
THE ELIJAH WOOD BRISKET

Here's a real treat if you happen to be entertaining fifty people or more. Feel free to adjust the amounts for days when you'd rather spend time with fewer people. This recipe comes from Jarrel 'Jay' Knowles from *aintitcoolnews.com* who along with son Harry and sister Dannie, hosted the gathering.

This was prepared for a film party in our backyard. It was eaten by Director Guillermo del Toro, Elijah Wood, Laura Harris, Josh Hartnet and about 40 others most of whom were working on *The Faculty* here in Austin. The party lasted till 5:45 am and there were no leftovers.

Preparation time for this was about 35 hours, 24 of those was spent with the meat soaking in my special sauce.

INGREDIENTS

25	links of fresh ground Meyer's Garlic Beef Sausage		24	ounces cheap Italian salad dressing
18	pounds Beef Brisket		24	ounces Guinness Stout
3	large red onions		⅓	cup fresh minced garlic
2	large green bell peppers		½	cup fresh minced rosemary
2	large red bell peppers		4	heaping tablespoons of course ground black pepper
6	dried and smoked chipotle peppers (cut in ringlets)			NO SALT !!!

DIRECTIONS

Combine stout, salad dressing, garlic, chipotles, and spices in a large pottery crock (the kind used in corning beef). Add the beef brisket and let soak covered at room temperature for about 3 or 4 hours.

While you're waiting, julienne the onions and bell peppers. Remove meat and lay brisket fat side down on your chopping block, run four lengths of hemp twine lengthways under the meat, cover the brisket with a thick layer of the onions and peppers (the thicker the better), fold or roll up the meat and veggies and bind tightly with the twine.

Stuff more veggies in the sides and place brisket back in the pot. Fill the space surrounding the brisket with the disconnected sausage links and over with leftover vegetables. Cover pot and place in fridge for about 24 hours. You'll probably have to remove a shelf. LOW-HEAT.

FAVORITE FOODS

Indian, South Chinese, a good steak

FAVORITE DRINKS

English bitter (beer), red wine, malt whiskey

I'll say that again: Low-heat. Smoke (I use Oak) the tied up brisket for about 6 hours, then bury it in sausage and smoke another 3 hours.

Remove from the pit, untie, and slice thinly across the grain. I had the soak'ns heating on the side of the pit all day to reduce it, I add the vegetables from the brisket to this and mix it up. Guests put sausage, brisket, and vegetables in whole wheat and flour tortillas adding jalapeños and Habanero Salsa to taste and pigged out.

In my cookbook this is called the "Elijah Wood Brisket" for our guest of honor that evening. You don't even need teeth to chew the meat it's so tender!

'Father Geek' aka Jay Knowles.

JEREMY BULLOCH
...ON FLYING FOOD

British actor and fan favorite Jeremy Bulloch got his start in Peter Yate's bubble gum musical *Summer Holiday* at the age of 17. He is now fondly remembered as Boba Fett in *Star Wars: Episode V – The Empire Strikes Back* and *Star Wars: Episode VI – Return of the Jedi*. Bulloch also co-starred in the popular British sci-fi TV series *Doctor Who* and *Starhyke* (2006).

ANECDOTE

The story I remember most was when I was doing a play and every night I had to eat a meal. One night whilst performing the scene where the cast was eating a three course meal, a piece of the food got caught in my throat. While I wasn't choking, I was still saying my lines with my eyes watering. All of a sudden I coughed and the piece of food lodged in my throat flew across stage and hit a member of the audience flush on her face. Needless to say the actors and audience laughed and the rest of the players performed with both us and the audience giggling like school kids. Luckily the play was a comedy. It was difficult to do that scene for the next few nights not to laugh when it was coming up to the next meal scene.

ALFRED HITCHCOCK'S
COLD VEAL AND HAM PIE

INGREDIENTS

¾ cup of beef lard   2 pounds cooked veal cubed

3 cups of flour   Veal drippings

½ teaspoon salt   1 pound cooked ham cubed

Butter   1 egg

         Milk

DIRECTIONS

Place the lard in a saucepan, with a pinch of salt. Bring to a quick boil for 3 or 4 minutes at medium heat. Stir in all at once, the flour, sifted with the salt, stirring constantly until the mixture leaves the sides of the pan. Remove from heat and continue to stir until the dough is cool enough to knead. Place the cooked dough on a floured board and knead it until it is perfectly smooth. Cover with a dry cloth and let it stand in a warm place for 30 minutes. Then knead again for 2 minutes.

Roll out two thirds of the dough and line a spring form mold with it. Fill it with the cooked veal and ham. Season with salt and pepper. Strain some of the liquid the veal has been cooked in and pour over the filling to within about one inch of the top. Dot the surface of the meat with small pieces of butter. Roll out the remaining dough large enough to cover the spring form and overlap the sides. Moisten the edges and crimp them together securely with the fingers. Make a hole in the center of the top crust and bake the pie in a slow oven (300°F) for 2 hours, brushing the top with the beaten egg mixed with a little milk, 30 minutes before removing from oven. Place in refrigerator for at least 6 hours before serving.

"MASTER WOULD LIKE MORE FAT."
- SEYMOUR KRELBOIN (JONATHAN HAZE)
THE LITTLE SHOP OF HORRORS (1960)

IB MELCHIOR'S
DANISH MEAT BALLS IN BEER

Born in Copenhagen, Denmark, Ib Melchior directed hundreds of early TV shows including Perry Como, before writing and directing science fiction films. Melchior is best known for his directorial work in *The Angry Red Planet* and *The Time Travellers*. Melchior resides in California.

Being Danish born I am partial to Danish food and libations, such as open-faced sandwiches and Aalborg Aquavit.

INGREDIENTS

3	tablespoons butter or margarine
1¼	teaspoon salt
1	onion, medium, chopped
1	pound finely ground lean pork
1	pound finely ground beef chuck
¼	cup flour
1	egg
¼	teaspoon pepper
¼	teaspoon nutmeg
1	cup milk
1	12-ounce can or beer
1	tablespoon lemon juice
¼	cup toasted bread crumbs

DIRECTIONS

Heat butter and ¼ teaspoon of the salt in a skillet, then brown the onion. In large bowl combine ground pork, beef chuck, flour, egg, remaining one teaspoon salt, pepper, nutmeg and browned onion. Mix well, adding milk slowly. Again mix very well and shape into tablespoon size balls and roll lightly in flour. Brown meatballs (called Frikadeller in Danish) in butter drippings, turning to brown evenly. When done add beer and lemon juice. Cover and simmer for 30 minutes. Serve hot, lightly sprinkled with toasted bread crumbs.

Serves: 4 to 6

The Missing Amoeba

After having directed about 500 live and filmed TV shows in New York including the *Perry Como Show* for three and a half years. My first feature motion picture as a director in Hollywood was a science fiction film called; *The Angry Red Planet*. There were two producers on the film: Norman Maurer, a talented and imaginative designer and one Sidney Pink. Mr. Pink was in charge of the purse strings and we were operating on a tight budget.

When the time came to shoot some important special effects, the money for it was gone.

One of the crucial effects was that of a giant amoeba oozing up an entire space ship, engulfing it. We literally had about $2.57 to do it! How?

Our local supermarket to the rescue.

We bought about $2.50 cents worth of Jell-O in various colors. We cooked it up in Norman's garage, which served as our studio for the project. We mixed it and used a small model rocket from the kids' toy chest, placed it on a hot plate and packed the Jell-O all around it. We then turned on the hot plate and the Jell-O melted down the side of the rocket ship. We shot it in reverse, and — presto — a giant amoeba engulfing a space ship, courtesy of the local super market.

The Jell-O also served in the close shot of the amoeba slithering over the space ship port hole, viewed from the inside. We poured the mess into a glass bottomed box, placed it across two ladders, and Norman shot it from below, while I "agitated" the Jell-O with my fingers. It worked. We did, however, not eat the Jell-O afterwards.

"AND AFTER THE STEAK, DO WE SEND SISTER TO THE MOVIES? TURN MOMMA'S PICTURE TO THE WALL?"
- SAM LOOMIS (JOHN GAVIN)
PSYCHO (1960)

JANET LEIGH'S
LAMB SHANKS

Born in California, Leigh is legendary for her role as Marion Crane in Alfred Hitchcock's *Psycho*. Leigh went on to do other horror films like *Night of the Lepus* and *The Fog*, but her career always comes back to that classic shower scene!

INGREDIENTS

4	lamb shanks		Celery seed (or salt)
1	sliced onion		Garlic, chopped
2	whole cloves	1	teaspoon ground ginger
2	tablespoons brown sugar		Dash of Worcestershiresauce sauce
2	tablespoons vinegar	½	cup red wine
Salt		1	can of mushroom soup
Pepper		1	can of celery soup

DIRECTIONS

Add two tablespoons of oil to a fry pan and brown the lamb shanks.

Pour off the fat and place in a crock pot with the rest of the ingredients.

Cover and simmer for about 6 or 7 hours on low heat.

If thicker gravy is desired, make a smooth paste with the following and stir in.

3 tablespoons water   3 tablespoons flour

Cook for another 30 minutes or until desired thickness.

"FACE-EATING, JACK? IS THAT SOME KIND OF A DELICACY?"

- WALTER (BRIAN DENNEHY)
COCOON (1985)

JOE DANTE'S
EDDY QUISTS'S HOWLIN' GOOD, LIPSMACKIN' RIBS

Born in Morristown, New Jersey, Dante originally worked for Roger Corman, who chose him to direct *Piranha*. Dante went on to direct many fan favorites including *The Howling*, *Gremlins* and *Innerspace*. Dante also directed the third segment of *Twilight Zone: The Movie* and television episodes of *Amazing Stories* and *Eerie, Indiana*. The *Masters of Horror* episode, "Homecoming" is Dante's latest work.

INGREDIENTS

2	pounds spareribs	½	tablespoon prepared mustard
½	cup molasses	¼	tablespoon salt
½	cup ketchup	¼	tablespoon pepper
½	cup onions, chopped	1	tablespoon bottled, thick meat sauce
1	minced clove of garlic		
3	whole cloves	½	tablespoon Worcestershire sauce
4	narrow strips orange rind-diced	¼	tablespoon Tabasco sauce
	Juice of half an orange		
1	tablespoon vinegar	1	tablespoon butter
1	tablespoon salad oil		

DIRECTIONS

Start heating the oven to 325°F. Place spareribs in shallow, open pan and cover with waxed paper or aluminum foil. Roast for 30 minutes. Pour off fat, roast for 30 minutes longer.

Meanwhile, make sauce. Combine molasses and rest of ingredients. Boil for 5 minutes. Pour off excess fat from ribs. Cover ribs with sauce. Increase oven heat to 400°F. Roast spareribs, uncovered, basting often for 45 minutes until fork tender, very brown and glazed.

To Serve: With scissors, cut spareribs into pieces.

Serves: 2 to 3

LON CHANEY'S
FAMOUS CHANEY POT

Son of silent film star Lon Chaney, Chaney started working in films after his father's death in 1930. He took small roles until his breakthrough in a touching performance as Lennie in *Of Mice and Men (1939)*. The following year he got the role that made him a legend as the sympathetic Lawrence Talbot in *The Wolf Man (1941)*. This was followed by a string of horror films for Universal studios and roles in the high profile hollywood pictures *High Noon (1952)* and *The Defiant Ones (1958)*. Chaney became a sturdy character actor in many low budget films later in his career and is beloved by fans today.

INGREDIENTS

4	pounds stew beef with bones	2	tablespoons oil
½	bushel beans	1	head cabbage
1	peck of potatoes		
4	small onions		**MUCHO SEASONINGS**
1	large celery stalk		(Mucho seasonings include:)
2	quarts corn		Salt
1	quart stewed tomatoes		Pepper
2	pounds carrots		Seasoned salt
1	pound peas		Beef bouillon

DIRECTIONS

Cook meat in oil until brown. Add 10 to 12 cups water and seasonings. Heat to boiling; reduce heat. Cover and simmer until beef is almost tender. Stir in chopped vegetables including beans, potatoes, onions, celery, corn, stewed tomatoes, carrots, peas and cabbage. Cover and simmer until vegetables are tender. You may adjust the recipe quantities to suit your taste.

Have fun with your own conversions of pecks and bushels.

Best enjoyed on a full moon.

ROBERT CLARKE'S
DREAM MENU

Robert Clarke started out as a contract player at RKO in mostly uncredited roles. He is known to fans for his parts in independent genre films of the 50's and directed the *Hideous Sun Demon*.

Vodka Martini to start

Basket of hot fresh bread

Caesar salad

Prime rib — medium rare

Stuffed potato

Asparagus

Decaf coffee

Chocolate sundae for dessert

The Devil's Messenger (1961)

The Haunted Palace (1963)

House of the Black Death (1965)

Dr. Terror's Gallery of Horrors (1967)

Spider Baby (1968)

Dracula vs. Frankenstein (1971)

SELECTED GENRE FILMOGRAPHY

ROBERT CLARKE (1920-2005)

TV:

Science Fiction Theater (1955)

Men Into Space (1959)

Kolchak: The Night Stalker (1974)

Beyond Westworld (1980)

FEATURES:

The Man from Planet X (1951)

The Astounding She-Monster (1957)

The Incredible Petrified World (1957)

From the Earth to the Moon (1958)

Beyond the Time Barrier (1960)

Alienator (1989)

Haunting Fear (1991)

Producer-Director-Actor:
The Hideous Sun Demon (1959)

RICHARD EYER'S
CYCLOPS STEW

Born in Santa Monica, Eyer worked in Hollywood as a child actor with such greats as Fredric March and Humphrey Bogart. Eyer is best remembered now as Baronni the Genie in *The 7th Voyage of Sinbad*. Eyer now teaches school and still makes the occasional appearance at science fiction conventions.

INGREDIENTS

4   pounds leg of Cyclops (OK to substitute 4 lamb shanks)

1   48-ounce can chicken broth

1   12-ounce bottle of your favorite beer (I use Corona)

1   large onion, sliced

1   cup celery, chopped

2   cups sliced fresh mushrooms

1   teaspoon crushed dry rosemary or 1 tablespoon, fresh minced

2   tablespoons crushed dry basil

8   cloves garlic, peeled and sliced (wards off giant birds)

1   bunch fresh cilantro (thick stems removed), coarsely chopped

Salt and pepper to taste

Potatoes (optional)

DIRECTIONS

Trim excess fat from lamb shanks and put in a crock pot with broth and beer. Add all other ingredients except garlic and cilantro. Cook on low setting approximately 9 hours. Add garlic and cilantro and cook an additional hour.

Serve over rice, white beans, or lentils. Or add potatoes to cook with stew for a complete meal.

SUSAN HART'S
DOROTHY NEIDHART'S JUNK

Born in Wenatchee, Washington, Hart appeared in an episode of *Alfred Hitchcock Presents*. Roles in *The Slime People, War Gods of the Deep* and *Dr. Goldfoot and the Bikini Machine*, both with Vincent Price followed. Hart now resides in California.

The following was my favorite dish as a youngster growing up in Wenatchee, Washington. In fact whenever my three sisters and brother reminisce about our childhood, one of us seems always to bring up the subject of "favorite things" mom would make," and "Mom's Junk" is at the top of the list.

And so now, whenever I find an excuse to "throw it together" (i.e. make something delicious in less than half-an-hour), I make "Dorothy Neidhardt's Junk," with good memories and much joy.

INGREDIENTS

1	large onion (any kind)	2 ½	cups cooked elbow macaroni
2	tablespoons oil (any kind)		
½	pound ground beef	1	can tomato soup

DIRECTIONS

Chop the onion. Heat the oil in the fry pan. Add the chopped onion, stir and cook until almost brown, then add the meat in small chunks into the onion mix. Add a little ground black pepper at this point if you wish. Cook until the meat is no longer pink. Now add the can of soup and about one third the can of water. Let simmer covered for about 5 minutes. Add the cooked macaroni, turn the heat to very low and let simmer covered another 5 to 10 minutes. Serve with a side of fresh fruit on a bed of lettuce.

Note: I always use an iron frying pan for this recipe. The only reason is that "that's what Mama used." But honestly, it does taste better... maybe it's that bit of iron seeping in? Voila! Junk!

SELECTED GENRE FILMOGRAPHY

SUSAN HART (1941-)

TV:

Alfred Hitchcock Presents (1962)

The Wild Weird World of Dr. Goldfoot (1965)

The Wild, Wild West (1966)

FEATURES:

The Slime People (1963)

War Gods of the Deep (1965)

Dr. Goldfoot & the Bikini Machine (1965)

The Ghost in the Invisible Bikini (1966)

It Conquered Hollywood! The Story of American International Pictures (2001) (as Herself)

JAY ROBINSON
...ON THE LACQUERED BEEF

Born in New York City, Robinson's quirky Broadway character work landed him a plum role as Caligula. Robinson has since made appearances in several sci-fi shows, including *Planet of the Apes* and *Star Trek*. Robinson, who now resides in California, is best known by fans as the host in *Beyond Bizarre*.

In *The Sword and the Sorcerer* where we were up at the Riverside Inn, there were four kings in the last whole sequence of the movie. I was one of the four kings and we sat behind this incredible banquet table with this great feast. There were hams, roasts, and piles of fruit like a medieval banquet.

Sure enough, we come on in front of these beautiful pork roasts for me to carve and eat at will. As the first day dragged into the second, then in the third, the flies came in earnest, and I have yet to have a bite of the roast. Pretty soon everything was inedible, as the shot was established and couldn't be changed to bring in another roast.

So there it sat, looking glorious on film but finally by the third day the odor was horrendous. They ended up spraying the roasts with some kind of lacquer to at least kill the odor. When I got home, after a few days filming at the Riverside Inn, what would you believe that my dear wife fixed for dinner but a lovely pork roast.

I immediately ran outside and said that it would be a long time before I could eat another bite of pork roast after what I'd been through. So here again, the food looked wonderful, but I couldn't eat it, as with *Planet of the Apes*.

In *Pee-Wee's Big Top* screening at the Academy, they told me it was a wonderfully funny sequence I was in. It was filmed at the Disney Ranch where the crew was falling down and could not stifle their laughter at my antics as the old red-neck fry cook. When we got to the theater for the screening at the Motion Picture Academy that night, my scene was cut almost entirely. Here I had invited all these big shot Hollywood types to see the screening and I got red faced because my scene was virtually eliminated from the movie. All you can see is me closing the window to the fry cookery.

EDGAR G. ULMER'S
TAFELSPITZ (BOILED BEEF)

INGREDIENTS

1½	pounds, lean, fine grained beef (brisket does fine)	½	bunch of parsley
2½	pints of water		SAUCE:
Salt		2	tablespoons horseradish
2	celery stalks	1	peeled grated apple
1	leek	2	tablespoons warm broth
1	bay leaf	Sugar	
1	carrot		

DIRECTIONS

Put the vegetables, cleaned and prepared in salted water and bring to the boil. Add the meat to the boiling liquid and allow slowly to cook until tender. Meat should always be covered with liquid

To make the sauce, combine all ingredients in a small bowl.

Serve with a hot vegetable, such as spinach or cabbage. The traditional way is to serve it with hot and/or cold chive sauce or the horseradish sauce.

TAG LINES

"I LOVE YOU. I WANT TO
EAT YOUR BRAINS."
- *THE RETURN OF THE LIVING DEAD (1985)*

"BACK WHEN YOU HAD TO BEAT IT
BEFORE YOU COULD EAT IT."
-*CAVEMAN (1981)*

BORIS KARLOFF'S STEAK AND KIDNEY PUDDING

Born in Camberwell, London, England, Karloff toiled as a stage and screen actor in the silent era of Hollywood before achieving everlasting fame as The Monster in *Frankenstein (1931)*. Karloff went on to star in many memorable fright films, including *The Mask of Fu Manchu, The Old Dark House, Bride of Frankenstein* and *Son of Frankenstein*. Karloff's last major film role was Byron Orlok in Peter Bogdanovich's *Targets*.

INGREDIENTS

FILLING:

2	pounds beef
6-8	kidneys
3	tablespoons flour
	Salt and pepper
1½	cups boiling water

CRUST:

8	ounces flour
1	teaspoon baking powder
1	teaspoon salt
8	ounces beef suet, finely chopped
½	cup warm water

DIRECTIONS

To make the crust, sift together into a large mixing bowl the flour, the baking powder and the salt. Add the beef suet and blend well.

Work in enough of the warm water to make a stiff but manageable dough. Roll out three-quarters of the dough on a lightly floured board.

Line a 4-pint pudding basin with the dough. Cut the beef into rather small ¾ inch cubes. Cut the kidneys in half and remove the white center core. Layer the bottom of the basin with the beef and kidneys. Sprinkle with flour and season with salt and pepper. Repeat with more beef and kidneys until you reach the top.

Fill with water to within an inch of the top. Roll out the rest of the dough and cover the top, tucking in well. Put several layers of waxed paper over the top and tie it on firmly. Place the basin on a rack in a large pan and pour in enough boiling water to come three-quarters of the way up the basin. Cover and steam for 4 hours.

Add more water occasionally as it evaporates.

To serve: remove the paper and cut a few gashes in the top for the steam to escape. Wrap a napkin round the bowl and serve.

Serves: 8

In the right weather this is a feast for the gods!

Photo is Boris Karloff and his daughter Sara.

BORIS KARLOFF'S
MEAT PASTE

Mix Coleman's Mustard (supersonically hot) with just enough Gin (not water) to make a paste consistency. Use sparingly with most meats.

PORK SHISH KA-BOB

INGREDIENTS

MARINADE:

2	large onions, diced
4	cloves of garlic, diced
¼	cup soy sauce
1	tablespoon fresh thyme
½	cup white wine
1	tablespoon fresh ginger, grated
½	cup molasses

SKEWERS:

4	pounds pork shoulder, cubed

Mushrooms

Peppers

Onions

DIRECTIONS

Combine marinade ingredients in a bowl. Place pork in a dish and pour marinade over top. Place in the refrigerator for at least an hour.

Place pork cubes on a skewer alternating with mushrooms, peppers and onions.

Grill on BBQ for 10-15 minutes.

ROBERT CORNTHWAITE
...ON "THE THING"

Born in St. Helens, Oregon, Cornthwaite a WWII Air Force veteran is best known for his work in *The Thing from Another World (1951)* and *War of the Worlds (1953)*. Cornthwaite continued to act in TV shows like *Men into Space, Thriller* and *The Twilight Zone* and his last horror film was *The Naked Monster (2005)*.

It's too long ago for me to remember what I ate in the RKO commissary in those days. Most of the stars ate in their dressing rooms, I imagine. But I remember William Faulkner daily at lunch, always alone at a middle table and occasionally Groucho Marx. I remember how Marx stared at me.

We had calling cards made up by the publicity department, reading "No, I am not the Thing!" I never passed one out; I threw them all away.

There's only one food story connected with *The Thing* that I can recollect. The publicity department set up a stunt in the Cut Bank, Montana, hotel where the company was staying. Someone bet that Douglas Spencer (Scotty in the film) couldn't eat a huge steak at one sitting! Doug loved steak and publicity, so he was glad to oblige them all by consuming a sirloin steak that draped over his plate at both sides, while photographers recorded it all. That's it. I'm sure the local newspaper ran the photos and the story, but I never saw them.

"YOU'RE COMING WITH ME. IT'S A LONG TRIP. I'LL NEED A SNACK."

- EDGAR
(VINCENT D'ONOFRIO)
MEN IN BLACK (1997)

LLOYD KAUFMAN
...ON KNOW YOUR INGREDIENTS II

In *Tromeo & Juliet*, we decided to add a head crushing at the last minute — we wanted the heroic, pedophilic priest to use his special blend of papal martial arts to step on and squash the skull of the goon, Vic. Because it was added to the script so late, the special effects artist, Louie Zakarian, wasn't prepared. The job was left to our harried prop artist, Samara Smith.

"But, Lloyd, I don't know how to make a fake head!" she said.

"Well, learn. dammit! All you need is some ground hamburger meat," I told her. Louie Zakarian, standing close by, shook his head in disdain.

"You can't do that. It's against everything I stand for," he muttered.

"Then make a new fake head!"

"I don't have the time, Lloyd. I have to finish Sammy's fake head by Tuesday."

"Fake heads!" I cried "Everybody's making such a big deal about fake heads! All you need is a tan balloon with a smiley face on it! It's the magic of cinema! These days everyone has to go around molding heads, applying real hair to the eyebrows. When I was a kid, we couldn't afford all that stuff."

Andrew Weiner, the Associate Producer, was standing by.

"When I was a kid, we were so poor we couldn't even afford real heads," he said. "We had to put big blocks of cheese on our shoulders. We couldn't see a damn thing. We'd be walking into walls. We also had to walk to school through the snow in our bare feet. These kids, they don't understand anything, do they, Lloyd?"

"That's hilarious, Andrew," I said. "You're fired." (Weiner actually went on to finish T & J but shortly thereafter went to work for Orion Pictures, where, coincidentally, cantaloupes run the company.) "Samara, just get the hamburger meat, some Karo syrup, and red food dye, and everything will be all right."

"A TASTY HORROR FILM!"

- MEATEATER, THE (1979)

"It's not gonna work," Louie said. "You got to have a brain, a cerebellum, an abscess behind the nose." But it did work, just fine. Samara took a head mold that had been discarded from Louie's workshop because it was covered with unintentional bubbles (it was a mold of the actor Patrick Connor's head, as opposed to that of John Fiske, the actor who was about to be killed — but what the hell, nobody would notice that). Samara filled it up with a mix of ground beef, Karo syrup, and red food coloring. We put the head on the floor, atop a pillow wearing the clothes John Fiske had been wearing in the first part of the scene (we made him wear a red bandana around his neck, to hide the split). We filmed the priest's foot squashing the head from two angles. The meat and goo spilled out from under the sides.

© *Troma Entertainment. Reprinted with permission of the author.*

BOB MAY
...ON GAME

Born in New York City, May is the grandson of Chic Johnson of the Olsen and Johnson comedy team. Trained as a dancer, he danced in several Elvis Presley films but is best known as the man behind the robot from the *Lost in Space* television series. May was the man behind the robot in every single episode.

For venison, I use a pepper-type rub and then throw it right on the barbecue. That is a hunter's dream. My wife Judy will marinate the venison for 24 hours. Then she adds herbs and red wine.

Judy will cook the venison in the oven about 325°F, which is very slow cooking, while basting it constantly. The slower the better, because then you get the aroma in your house. It drives you nuts! I will eat as much as my stomach will allow. We love to go out and get bear. A bear steak is like a sweet meat, which is very tender and very good. There's no cholesterol. Buffalo has less cholesterol than anything.

As a sportsman I won't go out there just to kill something. We don't like that. We enjoy the sport and the sanctity of the sport where you use everything. My wife's part native, so you use all the essence of the game and you don't waste anything.

DESSERTS

VERONICA CARLSON'S
NORWEGIAN APPLE CAKE

A striking blonde who went on to become a Hammer Films studio favorite, she is also known for her beautiful artwork rendered while working on and off the set. Carlson is now devoted to family and art and makes appearances at horror and science fiction film conventions.

For my wicket Stop Dodder.

INGREDIENTS

2	eggs	2	teaspoon baking powder
1½	cups superfine sugar	2	large apples
½	cup butter		Cinnamon
½	cup whole milk		Sugar
1⅓	cups all-purpose flour		

DIRECTIONS

Whisk eggs and sugar until whisk leaves a trail. Put butter and milk into a pan and boil. Stir boiling liquid into eggs and sugar. Mix in sifted flour and baking powder. Pour mixture into a large meat roasting dish, that has been buttered. Peel and core apples, slice and place on top. Sprinkle with sugar and cinnamon. Bake at gas mark 6, or 400°F for 20-25 minutes. Leave to cool in tin.

With love from your wicket Stop Murder.

This is a favorite family recipe. Recently, my step daughter asked for a copy of this, as she had mislaid the copy I'd originally given her — thus the "anguish languis" version of "Step Daughter" and "Step Mother."

"CARRIE, YOU HAVEN'T TOUCHED YOUR APPLE CAKE."

- MARGARET WHITE (PIPER LAURIE)
TO DAUGHTER (SISSY SPACEK).

CARRIE (1976)

DOUG BRADLEY'S
PINHEAD'S BIRTHDAY SURPRISE

Liverpool, England born Doug Bradley co-founded a theatre company with high school friend and renowned horror writer Clive Barker in the seventies. Bradley is adored by fans for his role as the menacing Pinhead in Barker's *Hellraiser* series. He has written a book *Monsters: Behind The Mask of The Horror Actor*, an historical treatment of movie monsters and the men who made them.

"It'll tear your taste buds apart!"

Food is something I take very seriously. I do a lot of cooking and like to think I'm pretty good at it. But rather than pass on one of my recipes, I thought it'd be fun to give you a dessert which my son Robert invented when he was 6 or 7 and which he called "Pinhead's Birthday Surprise."

INGREDIENTS

1 carton double cream	Ground hazelnuts
1 carton confectioners custard	3 bars of chocolate (1 milk, 1 dark, 1 white)
	Almonds, flaked

DIRECTIONS

Mix the cream and custard together in a bowl and add most of the nuts. Break up the milk and dark chocolate and melt it in a separate bowl over a pan of hot water. Add the melted chocolate to the cream and custard. Grate the white chocolate and sprinkle it over the mixture with the rest of the nuts. Refrigerate for 24 hours.

On serving, place a cleaned ½ eggshell in each bowl and fill with single malt whisky.

Enjoy...

...ON FOOD

Pinhead himself has never been a great one for culinary delights, though you'll recall him force-feeding the priest with his own flesh in *Hellraiser 3*! When we came to shoot the scene, some bright spark had thoughtfully provided

SELECTED GENRE FILMOGRAPHY

DOUG BRADLEY
(1954-)

www.dougbradley.co.uk

TV:

The Anatomy of Horror (Himself) (1995)

The 100 Greatest Scary Moments (Himself) (2003)

FEATURES:

Hellraiser (1987)

Hellbound: Hellraiser II (1988)

Nightbreed (1990)

Hellraiser III: Hell on Earth (1992)

Proteus (1995)

Hellraiser: Bloodline (1996)

The Killer Tongue (1996)

Hellraiser: Inferno (2000)

Hellraiser: Hellseeker (2002)

Hellraiser: Deader (2005)

The Prophecy: Uprising (2005)

Hellraiser: Hellworld (2005)

Pumpkinhead: Ashes to Ashes (2006)

raw liver for the actor to be given. Sliced peaches soaked in stage blood were quickly substituted.

I remember a wonderful meal I shared with Robert Englund in Madrid while we were filming *Killer Tongue* in 1995. The restaurant was called "Viridiana" and was full of stills from Bunuel's movies. I don't remember what we ate, but it was incredible. It's the only time I've seen red wine poured from a decanter through a candle flame to warm the neck of the decanter as it went. When the maitre'd realized who we were, he came over and proudly showed us his newspaper cuttings. *The Times of London* had rated it one of the ten best restaurants on the planet. Given that I had just insisted to Robert that this was on me, it was not altogether welcome news. Actually, for the quality of the food, it was amazingly good value.

Posh restaurants aren't really my scene though. Heaven for me would be one of those Italian lunches that last all afternoon, eaten outdoors at a huge table, surrounded by family and friends under a flower strewn pergola — fish, meat, pasta, fresh vegetables and fruit and lashings of red wine.

SUSAN GORDON'S
GOO CAKE

Here's a bit of movie "food" trivia for you: the red-colored "goo" that made the teenagers grow into giants in my father, Bert I. Gordon's film, *Village of the Giants*, was actually angel food cake with red food coloring, baked personally and specially for the film by yours truly, me. The goo was such a hit, the cast kept eating up the props and I had to bake a new "goo" cake every day!

We created our own version of the Goo cake. It's a simple to make treat served with fresh berries on the side and whipped cream.

INGREDIENTS

1 package angel food cake mix

2 cups bloody syrup (page 197)

DIRECTIONS

Follow package directions on the cake mix.

Follow the directions for the blood syrup but double the syrup and berries.

When done, heat sauce in pan until warm and pour over each piece of cake. Save some berries for garnish. Eat.

BEVERLY GARLAND'S
CHOCOLATE LADY FINGER ICE BOX CAKE

California born Garland appeared in many early 1950's sci-fi and horror films including *The Neanderthal Man*; *Curucu, Beast of the Amazon* and *The Alligator People*. Garland also worked in early TV shows like *Science Fiction Theater* and later the original *Twilight Zone*. Garland now resides in California and continues to run her own hotel.

INGREDIENTS

4	squares unsweetened chocolate	6	eggs separated
¼	cup water	1½	cup powdered sugar
1	cup granulated sugar	2	tablespoons vanilla
		2½	dozen lady finger cakes

DIRECTIONS

Melt chocolate (use double boiler) then add water and granulated sugar. When thick, add well beaten egg yolks. Allow to cool.

Cream butter with powdered sugar. Add the chocolate mixture to this with vanilla. Fold in stiffly beaten egg whites.

Line the bottom and sides of a greased 9 or 10" spring form pan with lady fingers and pour mixture into pan.

Arrange remaining lady fingers attractively on top.

Refrigerate overnight.

Serve topped with sweetened whipped cream and chocolate decorettes.

This has been a family favorite for years in our family. It came from my mother-in-law. It was years before she would give it to us. We love it.

SELECTED GENRE FILMOGRAPHY

BEVERLY GARLAND (1926-)

TV:

Science Fiction Theater (1955)

The Twilight Zone (1959)

Thriller (1960)

The Wild, Wild West (1965)

Planet of the Apes (1974)

Lois and Clark: The New Adventures of Superman (1993)

Teen Angel (1997)

FEATURES:

The Neanderthal Man (1953)

The Rocket Man (1954)

It Conquered the World (1956)

Curucu, Beast of the Amazon (1956)

Not Of This Earth (1957)

The Alligator People (1959)

Twice-Told Tales (1963)

The Mad Room (1969)

Hellfire (1995)

It Conquered Hollywood! The Story of American International Pictures (Herself): (2001)

MICHAEL CAINE'S
CARROT CAKE

Born in Rotherhithe, London, England, Caine was already an established star with *Alfie* when he made his first major appearance in a fantasy film, *The Magus* (1968). The ever adaptable Caine also starred in horror films including *The Swarm*, *The Island* and *The Hand* before acting in major television movies *Jack the Ripper* and *20,000 Leagues Under the Sea* (1997).

INGREDIENTS

2	cups plain flour	1	cup walnuts, chopped
2	cups sugar	1	teaspoon cinnamon
4	eggs	1	teaspoon ginger
¼	cup butter	⅛	teaspoon nutmeg
2	cups grated carrots (about 5 large carrots)		Vanilla essence
1	cup raisins	2	teaspoons baking powder

DIRECTIONS

Mix butter and sugar until creamy. Add one of the eggs and a few tablespoons of the flour. Then add the carrots in a mixing bowl and the rest of the ingredients. Bake for 40 minutes at 350°F.

"AH, THE GIRLS! LET THEM EAT A GUY NAMED 'CAKE.'"

- RAFE GUTTMAN
BORDELLO OF BLOOD (1996)

CANDACE HILLIGOSS'S
HEAVENLY TRIPLE CHOCOLATE CAKE

Born in Huron, South Dakota, Hilligoss is best known as the haunted Mary Henry in the original atmospheric cult classic *Carnival of Souls*. Hilligoss now resides in California and still makes the occasional convention appearance.

INGREDIENTS

1	8½-ounce box of deep chocolate or devil's food cake mix	½	cup toasted almonds (optional)
2	tablespoons cocoa	¼	cup mayonnaise
1	4-ounce box of instant chocolate pudding	4	eggs
¾	cup sour cream	3	tablespoons almond liqueur (like Amaretto)
½	cup vegetable oil	1	teaspoon almond extract
½	cup water	1	cup chocolate chips

DIRECTIONS

Preheat oven to 350°F. Grease 10 inch bunt pan with soft butter. Then dust with the unsweetened cocoa.

Place all ingredients except chocolate chips in large bowl and beat for 2 minutes with electric mixer on medium speed. Mix in chocolate chips by hand. Pour into prepared pan. Bake 50 to 55 minutes until cake tests done. If the toothpick you use for testing still has some wet chocolate on it, don't be alarmed. This is from melted chocolate chips not unbaked cake batter.

Cool on a rack for 10 minutes before removing from the pan. Place cool cake on a serving dish and drizzle with glaze. For the glaze recipe, mix all ingredients in a small bowl and let stand at room temperature until ready to use. Warning: if cake is still too warm, the glaze with disappear.

Glaze:

1	cup powdered sugar	1	teaspoon almond extract
		3	tablespoons milk

Once in a great while, when you tip the cake over onto a dish, a piece of the top may rip off. Sometimes, you can carefully scoop it up and repair it like a surgeon. If

SELECTED GENRE FILMOGRAPHY

CANDACE HILLIGOSS (1935-)

FEATURES:

Carnival of Souls (1962)

The Curse of the Living Corpse (1964)

Wicked (archival footage): (1988)

the damage is too great and can be seen by your guests, do this: Make a small dish of whipped cream, adding powdered sugar and vanilla extract.

Dab the top of the cake all around with whipped cream. Then decorate with large strawberries on top and also around the bottom at the sides. This makes the look of the cake even more sensational and creates a professional appearance that will have your guests believe a French baker was in your kitchen.

KEVIN McCARTHY
...ON FOOD

McCarthy is renowned by sci-fans as Dr. Miles Bennell in the original *Invasion of the Body Snatchers*. *The Twilight Zone* episode, "Long Live Walter Jameson" is one of many classic television shows McCarthy did. McCarthy, now in his 90's and still going strong, continues to attend conventions and has two new films on the horizon. He is author of the book *Invasion of the Body Snatchers: A Tribute*.

I like continental food, Italian food and French cuisine. I'm not that heavy on steaks and chops anymore as I used to be. I like a rissole. That's one of my favorite dishes. I like my wife making it. Kate makes her rissole and I eat it. She had variations on it.

In a restaurant I would order calamari, anti pasta so to speak and I might have a Caesar salad or veal scaloppini, if it's a very good Italian restaurant and knows how to cook it well enough to have a good scaloppini.

Like anybody else I might go into a fast food place, but instead of having a hamburger now, I'd have some sort of chicken meal.

I drink an awful lot of good wine. I drink a good deal of chateau, Candle Jackson's chardonnay. I like to have very valuable, more exclusive wines, but I don't know if I have the resources to keep buying wines at $80.00 a bottle.

I went to a lot of very good restaurants in Hollywood. I didn't go to Brown Derby. I went to Musso & Frank. They're a celebrated eatery on Hollywood Boulevard, been there for years and years. I might have a good lunch there with some of my friends.

Last night I ordered a very dry gin martini, with a twist of lemon and a couple of olives. I like chocolate sundae, but I don't order them anymore. I don't want to get too heavy. I'm always ready to take off another ten pounds!

TIPPI HEDREN'S
MARNIE'S RED VELVET CAKE

Born in New Ulm, Minnesota, Hedren is known best for her portrayal of Melanie Daniels in Alfred Hitchcock's *The Birds*. Hedren has also appeared in TV genre related shows like *Tales from the Darkside*, *Alfred Hitchcock Presents* and *The Bionic Woman*. Hedren continues to act and resides in California.

INGREDIENTS

THE CAKE:

½	cup shortening
1½	cups sugar
2	eggs
2	cups all-purpose flour
2	tablespoons cocoa powder
½	teaspoon salt
1	cup buttermilk
2	ounces red food coloring
1	teaspoon baking soda
1	tablespoon vinegar

THE FROSTING:

1	cup whole milk
4½	tablespoons flour
¾	cup butter
4½	tablespoons shortening
1¼	cups sugar
⅛	teaspoon salt
3	teaspoons vanilla

DIRECTIONS

Preheat oven to 350°F. Cream the shortening and sugar together until light and fluffy. Beat in the eggs. Sift together the flour, cocoa powder and salt and add alternately with the buttermilk and food coloring to the creamed mixture. Dissolve the baking soda in the vinegar and fold in. Pour batter into three greased and floured 8 inch layer cake pans. Bake 25 minutes, or until cake tester is clean. Cool on rack. Fill and frost with frosting

To make the frosting, gradually add the milk to the flour to make a smooth mixture. Bring to a boil, stirring until the mixture thickens. Cool. Cream the butter, shortening, sugar and salt together until creamy. Beat in vanilla. Combine the cooked milk mixture and creamed mixture. Chill and then use to fill and frost the layers. This makes about three cups of frosting.

RICHARD KIEL'S
JAWS DELIGHT CARROT CAKE

Kiel's towering 7 foot 2 inch frame enabled him to play several unusual roles such as the alien Kanamit in the classic *Twilight Zone* show "To Serve Man." Richard Kiel is best known as the nefarious 'Jaws' in two James Bond movies.

INGREDIENTS

2	cups sugar	2	cups shredded carrots
1½	cups oil	1	cup walnuts
3	eggs	1	16-ounce can crushed pineapple (in its own juice)
2	teaspoons vanilla flavoring		
2	cups all purpose flour	½	cup coconut
2	teaspoons baking soda		
1	teaspoon baking powder		**FROSTING:**
3	teaspoons ground cinnamon	1	pound powdered sugar
		8	ounces cream cheese
1	teaspoon salt	1	lemon

DIRECTIONS

Cream sugar, oil, eggs and vanilla. Mix in the flour, baking soda, baking powder, cinnamon and salt.

Stir in the carrots, walnuts, pineapple and coconut.

Pour cake batter into lightly floured pan(s) and bake in a 350°F oven for 35-40 minutes or until toothpick inserted in center comes out clean. Cooking time varies according to size of pan used.

Frost cooled cake with your favorite cream cheese frosting or use recipe below.

LEMON CREAM CHEESE FROSTING

Cream the sugar and cream cheese until light and fluffy. Add juice from one lemon as needed for desired taste and consistency.

Tastes best if frosted cake is placed in the freezer overnight, or longer as this improves the texture and makes the cake more moist. Be sure to cover the pan with aluminum foil.

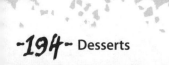

GEORGE CLAYTON JOHNSON'S
THE TOASTED HERSHEY SANDWICH

Born in Cheyenne, Wyoming, Johnson went on to write many classic episodes of *The Twilight Zone* and the original *Star Trek*. Johnson co-wrote the novel that became *Logan's Run*. *Ocean's Eleven* was based on an original story he wrote. The long haired, bearded writer makes occasional film and convention appearances and resides in California.

If you will believe it, I was once a teenager and in those days, I recall, it was a ritual to drive around, three or four guys in a car trying to pick up girls.

One of the regular pit stops was The Owl Inn, a late-night eatery with booths and a jukebox where you could get a burger and a coke, or, if you had been lucky enough to meet some adventuresome girls and wanted to impress them, you'd order a toasted Hershey sandwich and a strawberry shake, which was a house specialty designed for those who enjoyed a sugar rush, and could pay for it. The expensive entrée looked suspiciously like your familiar white-bread grilled cheese sandwich except that it would be oozing a rich brown instead of an orange-ish yellow.

The trick was turned by putting a couple of Hershey bars inside instead of the sliced process cheese, slathering the outside with butter and grilling it until sizzling brown.

Don't scrimp on the milk chocolate candy filling or run the risk of a bad trip. I have read somewhere that chocolate is an aphrodisiac. It didn't work on the girls we met — all it did was make them hyper.

" I'D COOK LIKE BETTY CROCKER AND LOOK LIKE DONNA REED!"
- AUBREY THE GIANT KILLER PLANT SINGING *LITTLE SHOP OF HORRORS (1986)*

SELECTED GENRE FILMOGRAPHY

GEORGE CLAYTON JOHNSON (1929-)

TV:

Alfred Hitchcock Presents (1955)

The Twilight Zone (1959)

Episodes:
"The Four of Us Are Dying"

"Execution"

"A Penny For Your Thoughts"

"A Game of Pool"

"Nothing In the Dark"

"Kick the Can"

"Ninety Years Without Slumbering"

Star Trek (1966)

The Twilight Zone ("A Game of Pool", 1989)

FEATURES:

Logan's Run (1976)

Twilight Zone: The Movie (1983) (segment 2: Kick the Can)

The Boneyard Collection (actor) (2006)

Logan's Run (2007)

DAVID HEDISON'S
OATMEAL COOKIES

Also known as Al Hedison, David began his career on the stage. A contract at 20th Century Fox, eventually led to starring in the genre classics *The Fly* and *Journey to the Center of the Earth*. But it was the hit TV show *Voyage to the Bottom of the Sea* that introduced him to a wider audience. Hedison, who changed his name in 1959, continues to work in movies and TV in California.

INGREDIENTS

½	cup safflower oil	¾	cup whole wheat pastry flour
¾	cup raw sugar or	½	teaspoon salt
½	cup honey	¾	teaspoon cinnamon
1	egg	1¼	cups rolled oats
1	teaspoon vanilla	½	cups raisins
½	teaspoon soda	¼	cup sunflower seeds

DIRECTIONS

Beat together the oil, sugar, egg and vanilla. Sift together the whole wheat pastry flour, soda, salt, and cinnamon. Add the sifted dry ingredients to the oil mixture. Stir in rolled oats, raisins and sunflower seeds. Drop onto baking sheet by teaspoonfuls. Bake in preheated 375°F oven for 10-12 minutes.

> "WHEN AN ARMED AND THREATENING POWER LANDS UNINVITED IN OUR CAPITOL, WE DON'T MEET HIM WITH TEA AND COOKIES!"
>
> - GENERAL EDMUNDS (GRANDON RHODES) LAYIND DOWN THE LAW
>
> *EARTH VS. THE FLYING SAUCERS (1956)*

FRIED BRAINS IN BLOODY SYRUP

INGREDIENTS

BRAINS

6   bananas, split lengthwise

½   cup brown sugar

½   cup maple syrup

2   tablespoons unsalted butter

¼   cup heavy cream

1   cup whipped cream

BLOODY SYRUP

½   cup maple syrup

1   cup of raspberries, fresh plus some for garnish

¾   cup blackberries

DIRECTIONS

BLOODY SYRUP:

Add berries to a saucepan and add the maple syrup. Cook on low heat until the berries are reduced by half. Strain to remove seeds and set aside.

BRAINS:

Add the brown sugar and the rest of the maple syrup to a clean pan stir until it starts to caramelize. Stir in the heavy cream and butter and stir until well blended.

Add the bananas to the pan and heat them in the caramel cream mixture until they are heated through.

To serve, place two banana halves with the caramel on a plate and cover with the berry sauce. Top with whipped cream and fresh raspberries for garnish and serve with a scoop of vanilla ice cream on the side.

BLOOD TRIVIA

Carrie (1976)

The pig's blood that was dumped on Sissy Spacek during the classic prom night scene was karo syrup and food coloring.

Dawn of the Dead (1979)

Much of the fake blood used in the blood packets was a mixture of food coloring, peanut butter and syrup.

Psycho (1960) & Night of the Living Dead (1968)

The blood is actually Bosco chocolate syrup.

BEST MEAL:

Bouillabaisse in Marseilles, France

FAVE FOODS:

Dumplings, lamb chops, beets, my mom's blueberry cheesecake.

KEVIN YAGHER
BANANA BRAINS

Illinois born Yagher, brother of actor Jeff Yagher, is the creative genius behind memorable horror characters Freddy Krueger makeup and the Chucky doll from the *Child's Play* films. Yagher, who has his own special-effects company, won an Emmy for his work on the *Tales from the Crypt* TV series. Yagher is married to actress Catherine Hicks (*Child's Play*) and resides in California.

There's a scene we did for *Starship Troopers* where Michael Ironside's character, Lieutenant Rasczak, discovers the dead body of a trooper. There is a large hole in the trooper's head from one of the bugs sucking his brains out. Mixed into the trooper's hair surrounding the hole is some blood and chunks of flesh. Lieutenant Rasczak reaches two fingers into the brain cavity and pulls out some mucous like brain matter. The brain matter and chunks of flesh were actually a mix of bananas and fake blood.

JESSICA RAINS
...ON LOST COOKIES

Whatever keeps the crew going: fried chicken, mashed potatoes and lots of it. Think of course, the actors are all dieting we need lots of salads and fat free entrees. And because my films are low budget, the cost is an issue. I had an actress who said she couldn't eat anything so we told the caterer to bring fruit and vegetables for the crew. For desert she brought fabulous toll house cookies.

When it came time to shoot a scene, I couldn't find the actress. She was locked in the bathroom eating the toll house cookies! Late at night I make brownies to keep everyone going. The hours are long and we have to constantly feed everyone.

> **"MILK AND COOKIES KEPT YOU AWAKE, EH SEBASTIAN?"**
> - TYRELL (JOE TURKEL)
> *BLADE RUNNER (1982)*

DOUGLAS FAIRBANKS JR.'S
PEANUT BUTTER FUDGE

New York City born Fairbanks, Jr. was known more for his romantic and classic film leads, but also starred in the rarely seen fantasy film *Outward Bound* (1930) and later the Peter Straub horror film, *Ghost Story*. Fairbanks Jr. was a naval officer during World War II.

INGREDIENTS

1½	cups milk	¾	cup smooth peanut butter
3	cups sugar	1	teaspoon vanilla extract
½	cup butter		

DIRECTIONS

Combine everything except vanilla, in saucepan or top of a double boiler. Bring to a steady boil, stirring to avoid scorching, especially if it's in a saucepan. Boil until a little of the mixture, dropped into cold water, forms a hard ball! Remove from heat and add vanilla. Beat until it loses its sheen (a long time!) then pour into a buttered, glass 13x 9x2 inch pan. Cool at room temperature, then cut into squares. Store airtight.

Note: Smooth Peanut butter seems to work best. The nuts in crunchy peanut butter lose their crunch.

Calories don't count!!! Enjoy.

SELECTED GENRE FILMOGRAPHY

DOUGLAS FAIRBANKS JR. (1909-2000)

TV:

ABC Stage 67 (The Canterville Ghost) (1966)

FEATURES:

Outward Bound (1930)

Sinbad the Sailor (1947)

Mister Drake's Duck (1951)

The Triangle (1953)

Ghost Story (1981)

TAGLINES

"IT'S SMOOTH AND CREAMY. IT'S LOW CALORIE AND DELICIOUS. AND IT KILLS. IT'S THE STUFF!"

THE STUFF (1985)

"THE ORIGINAL TASTY ENTREE!"

CRITTERS (1986)

FRED OLEN RAY'S
ATTACK OF THE 60 FT. SHOO-FLY PIE

Born in Wellston, Ohio, Ray a prolific writer, actor, producer and director keeps in shape by participating in ACW wrestling under the name Fabulous Freddie Valentine. Ray has developed many film projects including *Alienator* and *Ghost in a Teeny Bikini.*

INTRODUCTION

Back when I was much younger and working my way thru school as a security guard on the late night shift, I used to treat myself occasionally to breakfast at a Dutch-Amish family run hole-in-the-wall restaurant in Ft. Lauderdale, Florida when I got off duty. I used to like the fact that it smelled like my grandmother's kitchen back up in the hills of West Virginia. I guess some things just stick with you forever.

After having my usual breakfast I always had a dessert, even at 8 a.m., because this one particular restaurant served a home-made Shoo-Fly Pie, something that's darned near impossible to find anywhere! Shoo-Fly Pie, if you don't know, is a molasses confection that is an incredible treat, but really very rare.

Years later, now ensconced in Hollywood, after singing the virtues of my favorite lost dessert to anyone who would listen, a FedEx package arrived. Inside was — you guessed it — a fresh baked Shoo-Fly Pie, overnighted to me by the lovely JJ North, my well wishing star of *Attack Of The 60 Ft. Centerfold*. JJ was passing through some area of rural Pennsylvania, saw the pie for sale and kindly expressed it over to me. Now that's a pal!

She also sent a recipe for making one and I pass it along to you now. It makes two glorious Shoo-Fly Pies, so don't be bashful! Get started right away and if you're ever auditioning for me, well... you know what to do!

INGREDIENTS & DIRECTIONS

2	cups flour	¼	teaspoon salt
1½	cups brown sugar	4	tablespoon margarine

Mix together until crumbly. Take out 2 cups of crumbs for the top of the pies.

To remainder of crumb like mixture add:

2	beaten eggs	1½	cups hot water (not boiling)
2	cups molasses		

Mix well. Dissolve two teaspoons of baking soda in half cup of hot water and add to mixture. Pour into two unbaked pie shells and top carefully with reserved crumbs. Bake 450°F for 10 minutes.

Reduce heat to 375°F and bake for 30 minutes or until top is dry and done. If you're not really a molasses person, you can substitute one and a half cups of dark Karo Syrup, half cup of Light Karo Syrup, two teaspoons of vanilla extract and quarter teaspoon of maple flavoring, but why bother? It's perfect just the way it is!

"WAS SHE IN THE CAKE BEFORE YOU BAKED IT?"

- GOMEZ ADDAMS (RAUL JULIA) ENQUIRING ABOUT AN ABSENT DANCER FROM A GIANT CAKE

ADDAMS FAMILY VALUES (1993)

"HOW'D YOU LIKE SOME ICE CREAM, DOC?"

- DICK HALLORANN (SCATMAN CROTHERS) TELEPATHICALLY TO DOC (DANNY LLOYD).

THE SHINING (1980)

GENE AUTRY'S
PEANUT BUTTER PIE

Texan Gene Autry was a telegrapher before strumming his way onto the airwaves in radio and later film. Autry, known as the original "singing cowboy" only made one science fiction film, *The Phantom Empire*. Autry made dozens of westerns, served with the US Army during World War II. He retired to become owner of the California Angels baseball team.

INGREDIENTS

PIE:

1	cup peanut butter
1	8-ounce package cream cheese
1	cup sugar
2	tablespoons melted butter
1	cup whipping cream, whipped
1	tablespoon vanilla

CRUST:

1 ½	cups of graham crackers (about 7 double crackers)
¼	cup of melted unsalted butter

SAUCE:

4	squares unsweetened chocolate
1	cup milk
¼	teaspoon salt
2	cups sugar
¼	cup light corn syrup
2	tablespoons butter
1	teaspoon vanilla
½	cup sugar
1	teaspoon cinnamon (optional)

DIRECTIONS

Crush the crackers with a rolling pin or use a blender. Stir in melted butter and sugar and mix well. Press the mixture in the bottom and up the sides of a pie plate. Bake at 325 F for 15 minutes.

Cream together the peanut butter, cream cheese and sugar. Add the melted butter, whipped cream and vanilla.

Mix together well and pour into the crust. Chill 4 or 5 hours or until very well set.

To make the sauce: Heat milk and chocolate over low heat, and beat until smooth. Add salt, sugar and corn syrup. Bring to a boil and cook, stirring for 5 minutes. Remove from heat and stir in butter and vanilla. Store in the fridge. Can be reheated if desired. Makes two cups.

Top with melted, thinned hot fudge topping. Chill again about 30 minutes.

ANNE FRANCIS'S
EASY ICE CREAM PIE

Anne Francis starred in many Hollywood classics such as *The Blackboard Jungle* and *Bad Day at Black Rock*. She found a small but devoted audience in the short lived series *Honey West*. Fans remember her best as Altaira in *Forbidden Planet* or for her many television roles including *The Twilight Zone*.

Start with any kind of cookies you love. Any average package from the store will do. Chop them up in your chopping bowl, or however you do it, and add a stick of melted butter!

Mix well and make your crust in a nine inch round pie dish. Spoon in any kind of ice cream that you think will be fabulous with it and some chopped nuts or sauce (whatever you like). Put in the freezer using toothpicks and saran wrap to cover. Don't touch your great creation until it has frozen.

That's it... Keep the tums handy and enjoy.

FORREST J. ACKERMAN'S
DREAM BIRTHDAY CAKE

When I was middle-aged I told my friend the consummate cook, Anna-Marie Germeshausen, the kind of cake I would want for my birthday:

Bottom layer:

Vanilla Vanilla

Middle Layer:

Dream Dark Chocolate, Boston Cream Custard

Top layer:

Coconut Cake, Covered with Whip Cream, Topped with Shredded Walnuts

WOW!

SELECTED GENRE FILMOGRAPHY

ANNE FRANCIS
(1930-)

www.annefrancis.net

TV:

Lights Out (1949)

Alfred Hitchcock Presents (1955)

The Twilight Zone (1959)

The Man From U.N.C.L.E. (1964)

The Alfred Hitchcock Hour (1962)

The Invaders (1967)

Wonder Woman (1976)

Fantasy Island (1978)

Conan (1997)

Fantasy Island (1999)

FEATURES:

Portrait of Jennie (1948)

The Rocket Man (1954)

Forbidden Planet (1956)

The Satan Bug (1965)

Haunts of the Very Rich (1972)

Mazes and Monsters (1982)

Return (1986)

Love Can Be Murder (1992)

JAMES BERNARD'S
APRICOT SOUFFL

This is an impressive and almost foolproof soufflé

Ingredients

1 pound (or half a kilo) of dried apricots.

The whites only of 8 or 9 eggs (keep the yolks for something else)

Confectioners sugar, for dusting

Some good liqueur such as Kirsch or Cointreau — but this is not essential.

A small amount of unsalted butter

Directions

Put the apricots in a saucepan, cover with cold water, bring to the boil and simmer gently for about half an hour, or until the apricots are soft.

Puree the mixture in electric blender, tip into large bowl and add sugar to taste, usually quite a lot and a little liqueur if you wish. The result should be fairly thick. Allow to cool. All this can be done well in advance, even the previous day.

Heat the soufflé dish in the oven till the dish is thoroughly warm. Take it out and rub the sides and bottom quite liberally with the butter, using a knife or piece of grease proof paper. While the dish is still warm, scatter two or three large spoonfuls of sugar over the bottom, then lift it up and tilt it, turning it round and round, until the sides and bottom are well coated with sugar. This process helps to prevent the soufflé from sticking to the dish. Put the dish aside.

Whisk the egg whites, preferably with an electric beater, until they peak stiffly. You may find it easier to do this in two or three lots, to ensure complete beating.

Carefully fold in egg whites to apricots puree.

Put soufflé in a really hot oven about 400°F. The soufflé should then take about 20 or 25 minutes to rise and become nicely brown on top. When soufflé has reached its peak, remove from oven, powder the top with fine white sugar, put dish on a suitably large and attractive plate, and serve to, I hope, your wildly impressed guests.

Crisp almond amaretto or macaroons and glasses of sweet dessert wine make an excellent accompaniment.

Note: if I am serving this at a dinner party, I put the soufflé into the oven just as we are starting the preceding main course. The timing usually works out about right, but if you see that the soufflé is ready and the guests are not, simply turn the oven down low and the soufflé, which is an obedient one, will wait patiently without spoiling. Vice versa, if guests are ready but soufflé is not, I find well-fed people are quite happy to pause and chat and sip wine until the moment comes.

Don't worry if the soufflé is still slightly runny underneath. I think it makes it nicer.

Finally, what to do with the eight or nine egg yolks? I suggest making a real vanilla or chocolate ice-cream in the old traditional Italian way, or an iced zabaglione, or a crème brulee — but that is another, and very fattening story!

DESSERT SCENES

Bubba Ho-Tep (2002) – Elvis greets one of his impersonators eating a blueberry pie in this delightful off the wall horror superhero movie.

The Fly (1986) – Jeff Goldblum demonstrates the unsightly way flies eat donuts.

Braindead (1992) – Zombie mom eats custard… and more in this alternately gruesome and hilarious meal scene.

Harry Potter and the Chamber of Secrets (2002) – A cake magically dropped on dinner guests by an elf gets Harry sent to his room.

Rosemary's Baby (1968) – Chalky chocolate mousse served to Mia Farrow by Minnie Castevet (Ruth Gordon).

Young Frankenstein (1974) – Frankenstein, Igor and Inga are eating "Schwartzwald Kirchetort." The monster groans. Frankenstein (Gene Wilder) thinks Igor made a 'yummy sound.' The monster awakens.

Ghostbusters (1984) – Stay Puff marshmallow man terrorizes New York in the yummiest movie villain of all time.

Jurassic Park (1993) – In the middle of a power outage, John Hammond (Richard Attenborough) attemps to finish off ice cream as it -- and his dream -- melts away.

I, Robot (2004) – Det. Spooner's (Wil Smith) enjoys sweet potato pie made by his grandmother.

Indiana Jones and the Temple of Doom (1984) – Chilled monkey brains.

The Matrix Reloaded (2003): Merovingian (Lambert Wilson) contemplates, causality, the nature of the universe over a woman eating a chocolate cheesecake that induces an sexual pleasure after one bite.

JANE WYATT'S
GRANDMOTHER'S RICE PUDDING

Born the daughter of a Wall Street banker and a drama critic, Jane Wyatt was raised in New York City. She got roles on broadway and then on to hollywood where she became a contract player for Universal. She is best remembered as Margaret Anderson in *Father Knows Best* and in Frank Capra's *Lost Horizon*. She is known to genre fans as Spock's human mother on the *Star Trek* series and one movie.

INGREDIENTS

3 tablespoons rice

3 tablespoons sugar

1 teaspoon vanilla extract

4 cups milk

DIRECTIONS

Heat milk on low heat in saucepan. Add sugar and stir to dissolve.

Place milk mixture and the rest of the ingredients in oven proof dish.

Bake in 325°F oven for 2 hours.

Pudding will be creamy yellow with dark stain on top. It reduces a great deal.

OOPS!

In *The Truman Show* when Marlon is loading the candy machine, candy bars disappear.

Harry Potter and the Sorceror's Stone: Dudley eats Harry's birthday cake with his hands, but when he turns around, after Hagrid has given him a pig tail, there is no cake or icing on his hands or face.

The Incredible Shrinking Man (1957) A cake switches between Scott's left and right hands in two separate shots.

JOHN AGAR'S
BANANA BREAD

INGREDIENTS

½	cup butter	2	cups all-purpose flour
1	cup sugar	1	cup walnuts
2	eggs	Salt	
3	bananas, mashed	3	tablespoons buttermilk
1	teaspoon baking soda		

DIRECTIONS

Cream butter and sugar. Add eggs and salt. Add the bananas, milk, soda and walnuts. Mix well and then add the flour. Bake 45 minutes at 350°F. Test for doneness.

ALEXANDRA TYDINGS'S
CAKE SCENE

Originally hailing from Washington D.C. her first acting job was in the Royal Ballet's production of Isadora at the Kennedy Center at age eleven. She ended up playing bass for two punk bands and landing her role as Aphrodite in the television shows Hercules, and Xena. She currently lives in Los Angeles with her husband and children.

The photo at left was sent to us by Alexandra and is from the the Hercules episode "Stranger in a Strange World." It shows Alexandra as Aphrodite (left) and Lucy Lawless as Xea (right) after an ad-libbed cake fight. The ingredients curdled in the hot lights, and no one was willing to get near them.

SELECTED GENRE FILMOGRAPHY

ALEXANDRA TYDINGS
(1972 -)

TV:

Sheena (2000)

Xena: Warrior Princess (1995)

Hercules: The Legendary Journeys (1995)

JOYCE TAYLOR'S
ANTILLIA'S AMBROSIA

Born in Taylorville, Illinois, Joyce Taylor started her career with Mercury Records and eventually wound up under contract to Howard Hughes. Taylor is best remembered for her work as the gorgeous Princess Antillia in *Atlantis, the Lost Continent*. Taylor worked in Hollywood until the early 1970's and now resides in the Midwestern USA.

INGREDIENTS

Use equal amounts of any combination of fruits you enjoy I like:

Mandarin oranges

Seedless grapes

Apples, yellow and red

Bananas, peeled and sliced

Pears and pineapple

Miniature marshmallows

Sour cream, enough to mix and blend

Toasted coconut (optional)

DIRECTIONS

Cut the fruit into bite sized pieces and mix all the ingredients except the pineapple and coconut. Refrigerate the mixture overnight. Add the diced pineapple just before serving. The acid in the pineapple tends to break down the sour cream. Top with the toasted coconut and serve.

THE ONION KISS

Aboard the sailboat used in *Atlantis* were baskets of fresh food. Mr. George Pal, our director, writer, producer — a very sensitive, loving man — wanted to make the kiss in our love scene beautiful. Timeless, as he put it. But... before we did the shot, co-star Anthony Hall said, "I dare you take a bite of the fresh onion from the basket." I said, "You go first." He did, then I did, and then Mr. Pal walked onto the set, leaned close to us, and whispered his romantic directions. Breathing our onion breaths he said, "How could you? This is supposed to be romantic. You have ruined my favorite scene." He pulled away, hurt by our childishness. He returned shortly, took a bite of the onion, breathed into our faces and said, "Now let's do this love scene."

RAY BRADBURY'S
PEACH KUCHEN

Born in Waukegan, Illinois, Bradbury attended Los Angeles High School where he eventually met his life-long friends Ray Harryhausen and Forrest J. Ackerman, who made a pact deciding "they would never grow up." Bradbury, who wrote the screenplay for John Huston's *Moby Dick* and adapted his own novel *Fahrenheight 451* for Francois Truffaut, has since created some of the most memorable science fiction and fantasy works of all time.

INGREDIENTS

2	cups sifted all purpose flour	12	peach halves, fresh or canned or 2 packages of frozen slices
¼	teaspoon baking powder	1	teaspoon cinnamon
½	teaspoon salt	2	egg yolks
1	cup sugar	1	cup heavy or sour cream
½	cup butter or margarine		

DIRECTIONS

Start your oven at 400°F or moderately hot and get out an 8-inch square pan. Sift flour, baking powder, salt and two tablespoons sugar together in a mixing bowl.

Cut in butter or margarine with two knives or a pastry blender until mixture looks like coarse cornmeal. Pat an even layer of this crumbly pastry over bottom and halfway up the sides of baking pan. Use your hands and press firmly until it holds.

Skin fresh peaches and cut in half; drain canned; thaw and drain frozen peaches. Arrange peaches over bottom of pastry neatly and sprinkle with a mixture of remaining sugar and cinnamon. Bake 15 minutes, then pour a mixture of slightly beaten egg yolks and heavy or sour cream over the top. Bake 30 minutes longer. Serve warm or cold.

Serves: 6

If they don't have this on Mars, I don't want to go there.

"EAT YOUR PUDDING, MR. LAND."

- CAPTAIN NEMO
20,000 LEAGUES UNDER THE SEA (1954)

VAL GUEST'S
STICKY TOFFEE PUDDING

Genre fans know Guest for the quintessential British science fiction classics *The Day the Earth Caught Fire*, and *The Quatermass Experiment*. Guest completed his autobiography, *So You Want to Be in Pictures (2001)*.

INGREDIENTS

PUDDING:

4	tablespoons softened butter
¾	cup granulated sugar
2	cups flour
1	teaspoon baking powder
1	egg
¾	cup stoned dates
1	cup boiling water

1	teaspoon baking soda
1	teaspoon vanilla essence

TOPPING:

4½	tablespoons brown sugar
3	tablespoons butter
2	tablespoons heavy (35%) cream

DIRECTIONS

Cream the butter and sugar together. Sift the flour and baking powder. Beat the whisked egg into the creamed mixture with some of the flour. Continue beating for a minute or so before mixing in the rest of the flour.

Flour the dates lightly and chop them finely. Pour the boiling water over them.

Mix in the baking soda and vanilla. Add this mixture to the batter and blend well. Turn it into a buttered 11x7 cake tin. Bake for about 40 minutes in moderate oven 350°F (Mark 4).

For the toffee coating, heat the brown sugar, butter and cream and simmer for 3 minutes. Pour over the hot pudding and place under hot grill until it bubbles. The coating burns easily so be sure to check after a minute.

INGRID PITT'S
VISCERAL DELIGHT

INGRID PITT'S SPECIAL PUDDING

The ingredients are all easily acquired on a mid-night shopping spree but don't forget to get your more perishable goods in the freezer by dawn even if it does mean defrosting the odd limb or two you have been saving for that special occasion.

A Hand of Gloryful of eggs, preferably stolen from a graveyard at the full of the moon. (Or Teso's, if you are really into the black arts).

Sweeten their destruction with three quarters of a small skullcap of sugar and dust with an eye-socket of Cinnamon.

One and a half cups of bread crumbs filched from an Irish Wake.

Half a skullcap of butter melted over a well-heated torture brazier until it's thick and warm and as runny as a grave diggers left nostril.

One pound of stoned Morello Cherries (If you can't find them stoned, brandy sozzled will do.)

And a little mixed skin (If you can't get the real thing try lemon and orange but...)

What you do is this. Wrench the unformed foetus (yoke) from its food source (albumen), feed it the sugar to lull it into a false sense of well-being and then beat it into submission. Smother it with the milk, cinnamon and bread crumbs. It should be groggy now and be prepared to accept the hot butter.

Dump the cherries into the gooey mess and pitch in the fruit skins for good measure. Beat the egg whites until they can barely stand up in the bowl and then secrete them away in the visceral mess. Grease a souffle dish, defile it with the bread crumbs and seduce the mixture into the bowl.

Without waiting for a reaction, slam the bowl into a moderately hot bonfire, preferably on an adjacent cross roads or, alternatively, into an oven at 180 degrees C (350°F) Mark 4 and resist all pleas to remove it until it turns a Mummy brown colour and has done a Dracula and risen. But Beware! This dish is addictive!

TURHAN BEY
...ON HIS FAVORITE DESSERT

Turhan Bey moved to the United States in 1930 where he steered towards acting. Bey enjoyed enormous success in the 1940's adding international flavor to eerie and villainous character roles. He is known to fans for *The Mummy's Tomb* opposite Lon Chaney Jr. and for his leading role in *The Amazing Mr. X*. He returned to Vienna after the war and made a name for himself in photography. Bey made something of a comeback later in life and garnered a whole new generation of fans with this roles in the television shows *Babylon 5* and *SeaQuest DSV*.

My favorite dessert is the Fächertorte which was a popular dessert in Vienna before the war. During the war, the ingredients were scarce so it was hard to find but after the war some cafes brought it back. I usually find it in the Demel cafe in Vienna. The dessert consists of a layer of pound cake, hazlenuts. The next layer is poppy seeds, honey and then more cake and lemon. Then a layer of apples with cinnamon and raisons and more lemon juice. The entire cake is covered in a bread like crust that's more like shorbread.

CONTRIBUTOR INDEX

RECIPE INDEX